ROCKET SCIENTISTS' GUIDE

TO MONEY AND THE

ECONOMY

MIKE SOSTERIC

Version 1.0

I'll tip my hat to the new constitution
Take a bow for the new revolution
Smile and grin at the change all around
Pick up my guitar and play
Just like yesterday
Then I'll get on my knees and pray
We don't get fooled again.
The Who

ROCKET SCIENTISTS' GUIDE TO MONEY AND THE ECONOMY

ACCUMULATION AND DEBT

MIKE SOSTERIC

Lightning Path Press
St Albert, Alberta. Canada
press.lightningpath.org

©2016 Lightning Path Press.
All rights reserved.

Print ISBN 978-1-897455-11-1

eBook ISBN 978-1-897455-18-0

Table of Contents

INTRODUCTION

Money, money, money.

Money makes the world go round, so what is the problem with money? Well, money is the root of all evil, or so we are told. It is the bane of our existence. It is the source of our despair, especially if you don't have it and therefore can't buy enough to eat.

Money, money, money.

Money is bad, and that is the bottom line.

But is money really bad? Personally, I do not think so. Consider my own work; consider this book. As a writer of my ilk writing a book of this nature, I have often been approached by people suggesting that I should give this book away for free. It is a critical book they say, and it is an important book, so shouldn't you make it freely available? After all, you can't charge for something as basic and important as this information, right?

The question always bothers me and sets up a bit of a conflict. I agree with the sentiment, to a degree. The information that I provide should be accessible to everyone who wants it; but should it be free? Personally, I do not think so. Having spent thousands and thousands of hours writing, it seems disrespectful and insensitive to ask someone something like that. You do not go up to the baker of your daily bread and say, "hand over the bread 'cause I'm entitled", do ya?

Of course not!

To do that would not only dishonor and disrespect the work that the baker put in, but it would be insensitive to the fact that in this western world you cannot do anything without money, you cannot even eat. I mean, I live in a nice house, but I cannot grow food where I live because I couldn't afford a yard big enough to grow food. What is worse, because of the way the global economy is set up, I cannot even **barter**[1] my services. How am I going to barter my English writings and books for bananas grown by a Latin American field laborer, or clothes sewn by a Chinese worker in a factory? The truth is, I cannot.

If I do not make money from the work I do (which is to write useful and interesting books), my family and I do not eat. In this day and age, we all need money to survive and so no, I shouldn't be required to give my labor away. Still, as I said, I do agree with the basic sentiment. The bottom line is, everybody who wants to buy my books should have the money they need to do so. That everybody doesn't have enough money to buy my books is the basic issue and fundamental economic problem of this planet.

So you see, the problem is not that I do not give the information away for free, and the problem is not money itself. As we will see in the main body of this essay, money itself is good, and having money is good as well. The problem is, the evil is, not having enough money to survive. The problem is that despite the fact that we (and by "we" I mean the people of this Earth) have amazing technology and amazing productive potential, not everybody on this earth can afford the modest fee I charge for my books. Considering how little I'm asking (basically a couple bucks

[1] See http://spiritwiki.lightningpath.org/Barter.

a book in some cases), it's a crime, and it's a crime that goes way beyond the desire to have information available for free. I mean, it's not just books that people cannot afford. Many people on this earth do not even have the money they need to buy food and decent shelter and because of that, a lot of children on this earth go hungry and starve. Considering our modern productive capacity (which is massive), and considering that (once we eliminate overconsumption, unnecessary consumption, and waste) there is more than enough food and resources to go around for everybody, letting even a single individual, let alone a child, starve because they do not have enough money is a crime of truly biblical proportions.

So, the problem on this Earth is not with money itself (money is good because, as we will see in some detail below, it helps us exchange), the problem is that people do not have enough money. In this context the question is not, "Is money evil?" or "How do we give things away for free?" In this context, the question is why do so many people lack the cash they need to buy the things that they want even when there is way more than enough food, clothing, and shelter to go around?

THE NATURE OF MONEY

To answer the question why people do not have enough money, you first have to figure out what money is, and that is very easy. Let us start by saying that money is not the paper it is printed on. Money is not gold, it is not silver, it is not platinum, and it is certainly not a shiny diamond rock you put on your finger to impress your family and friends. Money is not a concrete thing at all. In fact, when you think about it, money is simply an idea, and it is an idea that, despite what some people might want you to think, is not that hard to understand. It is simple, really. When you boil it right down to its essence, *money represents time.* Time is money they say, and that's totally true; though to be honest there is a bit more to it than that. Money does represent time, but not all types of time. Money has a very specific reference and that is work. We can say that *money represents work time.*

When you think about it like this, it seems rather obvious. You work an hour; you get paid for an hour. If you stand around and do nothing, money does not fall from the sky. You only get money when you work. Therefore, money is work time; but even that is not wholly specified. While it is true that money does represent work time, it is also true that money doesn't represent all types of work time. Money represents a very specific type of work. The fact is, I do not get paid money for working in my backyard; I only get paid money when I'm doing something for somebody else. When I do something, build something, or provide a service for somebody else, I get money in exchange. Although I might fantasize about it, you the reader are not going to give me a single penny for working in my garden to grow flowers for my kitchen table. However, I might be able to convince you to give me a few pennies for a flower I've grown for your kitchen table.

You see how that works?

Money, money, money.

The definition of money is this: money represents time spent working for someone else. If we define "time spent working for someone else" as **labor time**, then we can say with clarity and specificity that **money equals time spent laboring for other people**. Put it in a formula and it looks like this:

$$Money = Labor\ Time^2$$

Or

$$Money = the\ time\ you\ spend$$
$$working\ for\ another\ person$$

See how simple that is!? Money = Labor Time. And now you know what money is.

THE ECONOMY

The whole money = labor time thing should be obvious to you at this point, but the understanding this gives you is still basic. To get a better idea of what money is all about, we have to take a look at money in an **economy**.[3] Once again, that is easy. An economy is simply the formal exchange of something. Whenever two or more people get together

---

[2] http://spiritwiki.lightningpath.org/Labor_Time.

[3] http://spiritwiki.lightningpath.org/Economy_

and do something for each other in exchange for something else, you have an economy. Thus, if you come over and clean my windows and I give you a loaf of my home baked bread, we have exchanged something (you have exchanged labor for my bread) and we have an economy. Simple! Understanding money in an economy is equally simple. Since money = labor, an economy where money is exchanged is essentially an economy where labor is exchanged.[4] We can express that in a formula thus:

Economy = Labor Exchange

As you can see from this, an economy is a fundamentally social thing. *Economies emerge out of human interaction and are designed to fulfill human needs.* When you are engaged in economic activity, you are working for, and with, other people in order to meet your needs (e.g., a need for clean windows, a need for bread, etc.). No social activity? No social exchange? No economy!

Now of course, there are different types of economies and not all economies need money to function. That is, not all economies are **monetized.**[5] In our modern world, the **official economy,**[6] that is the economy that is recorded, monitored, taxed, and fiercely policed by those in power, does use money and is therefore monetized. Beneath that official economy however there are other economies.

---

[4] Remember, labor is what you do when you work for someone else.

[5] A monetized economy is simply an economy that uses some form of abstract currency, rather than barter, for exchange. See http://spiritwiki.lightningpath.org/Monetized_Economy.

[6] http://spiritwiki.lightningpath.org/Official_Economy.

There is the underground economy, for example. The **underground economy** (the black market as it is sometimes called) is also a monetized economy, but it is not recorded and taxed like the official economy. Alongside the underground economy there is also the **informal economy**.[7] The informal economy uses barter as a method of exchanging labor. When I traded a complete set of my books to a young man who helped to clean the windows in my house there was an exchange of labor, but it wasn't monetized, it was barter. The point here however is not to go into detail about the different types of economies; the point is simply that an economy involves the exchange of labor. Whether that labor is represented by money or barter, or is recorded or not, is irrelevant. The simple truth is this: an economy involves the exchange of labor.

We can see this quite clearly if we simplify things by looking at a small economy of only one hundred people. In this simple economy, everybody does something useful for somebody else. One person plays guitar, another sings, another builds houses, one runs a farm, another is into computers, another bakes bread, another processes animals, and so on. They all have a skill (or skills), they all have things they love to do, and they all get up every day and apply those skills in their daily life. In our small economy of one hundred people, each individual has some specialized talents and abilities and they bring these talents and abilities to their community; and that is great because not everybody is the same. Not everybody likes to build things, not everybody likes to sit all day and write, not everybody likes animals, and so on. However, that is OK

---

[7] http://spiritwiki.lightningpath.org/Informal_Economy.

because in an economy we can all get what we need (and want) by exchanging with each other for things that we cannot (or will not) do ourselves.

As noted above, there are different ways of exchanging labor. Barter (i.e. I build you a house, you give me a lifetime supply of hamburgers) is fine as far as it goes, but it is quite limited because barter is neither an efficient nor a flexible means of exchanging labor. The problem is, you may not want what the other person has to barter. Maybe I'm a vegetarian carpenter and you are a butcher. If so, how are you going to trade with me? Or, maybe you the butcher already have a house and do not need the services of a carpenter, or a plumber, or an electrician. If so, how are the plumber and electrician going to eat?

You see the problem?

Barter is inefficient and inflexible.

Enter money.

Money, money, money.

Money is a medium for exchanging labor power, but it is an abstract medium. Money doesn't represent a specific type of labor (i.e. carpentry) or a specific type of product (i.e. hamburger), money represents all types/any type of labor. Money is labor power abstracted and as abstracted labor, **money lubricates economic exchange!** If I spend an hour building a house for you, instead of giving me hamburger meat (which I do not like) you will give me some money to represent my labor. This is great!! If you give me some money to represent my labor, I can then use that money to buy something that I do like (i.e. fruits and vegetables) from somebody else.

14

Isn't that cool?

With this in mind we can now refine our definition of money and say that...

Money = Abstracted Labor Time

As you will no doubt conclude, *money is a major improvement over a system of barter because it abstracts labor.* When the economy is based at least partly on money (i.e. partly monetized), then your options for exchange are expanded and any problems that might exist (like a vegetarian trying to trade with a carnivore) simply evaporate. Instead of paying me in dead meat (which I, as a vegetarian, would never accept), you can now pay me cash. This is fantastic because now I can buy whatever I want with no worries. And the benefits of money go way beyond simply lubricating exchange between vegetarians and carnivores. As an abstracted measure of labor time, money makes economic exchange more efficient, flexible, and fluid. In a monetized economy, all the inefficiencies, obstacles, and hurdles of barter simply evaporate. Indeed, and as we will see, monetized economies are what make the productive potential of modern societies possible. When money is in play, and in particular when money is backed by modern communication technologies, you can exchange labor with anybody, anywhere in the world, with magical facility and grace.

But, I'm jumping ahead. The point here is simply this: money is simply abstracted labor time. Money allows us to exchange labor time with each other in an efficient and fluid way. Put this way, money hardly seems like the root of all evil as so many people like to think. Put like this, it would seem that money is a good thing after all.

THE SOURCE OF MONEY

If money is abstracted labor, and if the economy is nothing more than a way to exchange labor, then where does money come from? Well, it does not, normally, appear out of thin air. Money comes into being in a two-step process. **First**, somebody makes it. If it is paper money, we put paper through a press with special inks and we print it. If it is metal money, we stamp it with a logo and some numbers. **Second**, we agree on a value. It is as simple as that. It is important to note, whatever you are using for money, whether it is gold, lead, or stone, does not matter. All that is important is that the people who are involved agree that this piece of paper, that lump of metal, this other shiny sparkly rock, or that new tulip bulb,[8] represents a certain amount of labor time. That is all there is to it. Once you agree that you are going to abstract labor and pour it into some kind of container, all you need is a container to attach it to, general agreement about the value of the container, and voila, you have money. It is all a question of concordance. If I hand you a piece of blue paper and tell you it's worth one thousand labor units (assuming one

---

[8] The fact that value/money is created by general collective agreement is brought home by Tulip Mania. Tulip mania was a period in Dutch history (whose peak was in 1637) where the humble tulip bulb became extraordinarily valuable. At one point, according to the stories, a single tulip bulb could be used to buy 12 acres of land! This is now known to be an exaggeration, but there is no doubt that tulip bulbs were extremely valuable for a short period in Dutch history. They were extremely valuable because of concordance; people agreed that they were valuable, and so they were. For more see
https://en.wikipedia.org/wiki/Tulip_mania.

labor unit is one hour of labor) and you agree, then we have
created money.

THE VALUE OF MONEY

I suppose the question that arises now is, how do we
determine the value of money? That is, how do we
determine how much labor power is represented by our
instruments of exchange? Obviously, the value isn't
intrinsic to the instrument. That is, a piece of paper isn't
automatically worth one thousand labor units. Indeed, a
small piece of off-white paper printed in a huge mill with
automated machinery at economies of scale is probably
worth something in the order of .001 cents. The same can
be said of other instruments of exchange, like the gold,
silver, and diamonds that have been made to hold value
over the centuries. No matter what anybody tells you, gold
has no **intrinsic value**.[9] It has a small **labor value**,[10] but it is
worthless over and above that. It is only when we agree that
gold, paper, shiny rocks, or whatever are worth "something
more" that they take on a **monetary value** over and above
the value of the labor that went into producing them.

Of course, the question at this point is, how do we add
monetary value to money? As noted above, *the monetary*

---

[9] In the context of this discussion, putting an economy back on a
"gold standard" makes absolutely no sense at all.

[10] The labor value of something is the total amount of labor that
went into producing and distributing the item for exchange. The
labor value of gold is the total amount of labor that went into
extracting it from the ground, refining it into purity, shipping it to
the store, forming it into a ring, and putting it on a finger.

value of money is derived simply from the amount of value that we agree it represents. Since, as we have seen, Money = Labor Time, the value of any piece of money is the value of the *labor time* that it contains. Since the value of money is determined by concordance, the labor contained in any piece of money is determined by agreement. If you and I agree that a piece of paper with a certain president's head on it is worth 10,000 labor-units, then so it is.[11] As such, we may say that the value of money is the **labor-exchange value**[12] (or just **exchange value** for short) that it has. If you can exchange a certain paper bill for ten hours of labor, then the labor-exchange value of that bill is ten (labor hours).

So, money contains the amount of labor that we agree that it contains. Clearly however we just don't make up a value and assign that. That is, the value of money is not random,

---

[11] Of course, you and I do not agree to the value of money. Money is too important to be left up to the random decisions of a billion people. Instead, the value of money is determined centrally by the people (we might call them the players) who control the money supply. These people print a dollar bill, give it a number, tell you what it is worth, and you agree. Understand, this is not necessarily a bad thing. In a free an open system where everybody understands the purpose of money and where money is implemented as a means of equitable and efficient labor exchange, knowing the value of money is critical. The problem comes, as we shall see, when the economy is twisted and corrupted in the interests of a few. When the economy is twisted and corrupted to benefit the few (as it has been for thousands of years now), the central assignation of value becomes twisted and corrupted as well.

[12] http://spiritwiki.lightningpath.org/Labour-Exchange_Value.

or at least, it shouldn't be. Technically *the value of money, or more accurately the total value of all money in a given economy, should be determined in relation to the total amount of labor being exchanged in an economy.* That is, all the money in a society should be approximately equal to all the labor that is available to exchange. We could say that...

Total Value of All Money to Exchange (ME) =
Total Labor Available to Exchange (LE)

I know the above might sound complicated, but it is not. A simple example will suffice to bring clarity. Say you have a small economy of one hundred people and you want to monetize (i.e. add money in a way that displaces barter as a primary form of exchange) that economy. How much money will you introduce? Well, you want to introduce exactly as much money as will represent the total labor output of the one hundred people in the economy. For example, if you measure each hour of labor as one unit, and if most people work four hours a day, seven days a week, then in order to fully monetize our little economy you would add one hundred and forty-six thousand (146,000) units of labor. That is four hours a day (4), times three hundred and sixty-five (365) days a year, times the one hundred (100) working people in the economy. If you did that, if you added enough money so that ME = LE you would have a fully monetized economy with enough money circulating so that everybody could freely (and fairly) exchange their labor!

As for individual pieces of money, their value should be determined in relation to the total value of money in the economy. Assuming you are starting fresh and with no history of inflation, how much an individual piece of money is worth would depend on what fraction of the total it represented. If you wanted to you could circulate the required 146,000 units of money in our small economy using 146 thousand-dollar bills; in that case, each bill would be worth 1,000 labor units. Alternatively, you could break it up and circulate it as 146,000 one-dollar bills. In that case, each bill would be worth one labor unit. Of course, a combination of big and little bills, small coins and other containers is probably best. Regardless of what you choose, the value of the individual bills is only meaningful in relation to the total labor output in an economy. In other words, in order to determine the value of money in an economy, you have to look at the amount of labor in the economy (i.e. the number of people working and the hours they work) as a whole, estimate that, and then create enough money to serve in the interests of exchange.

And that, my dear friend, is money. Money is abstracted labor-time; money is used to lubricate economic exchange; money has value because we all agree that it does. Finally, the value of all money in an economy should be determined by the amount of labor that needs to be exchanged.

Voila!

I am sure you will agree, this is all very simple. Indeed, at this point, you should have a clear understanding of the nature and purpose of money. At this point you should also see that **money is a good thing**. *Money is a way to lubricate [social] exchange and so money is not inherently evil, it is inherently social.* I would even go so far as to say that money is inherently spiritual. I would say this because money facilitates individual and collective creation, and positive and life-affirming creation is what Spirit is all about. Looking out and seeing all the evil, greedy, and anti-social uses to which money is put may cause you to doubt what I say, but it is not money per se that is the cause of all these evils. Rather, and I will explain this a bit more later on in this essay, all the evils of the world are caused by **disconnection**.[13] Money, as we shall see, only facilitates evil; and, it does this only because it facilitates the accumulation and control of labor power! Money could just as easily facilitate good. As we will see in the rest of this essay, it is the "love of money" (or rather, the love of what money gives you, which is power over others) coupled with the easy way money can be accumulated that is the cause of all our local and global problems.

But, I'm jumping ahead. Now that you know what money is, it is time to turn to a discussion of the problems associated with money. As we will see, there are some "doozies." While it is true that money makes the modern world go around, and while we could easily (and accurately) say that without money we could not have built our wonderful modern world, it is equally true that there is something about money that is rapidly bringing our world to a cataclysmic end. The truth is, we as a human race face an increasingly dire situation. As should be obvious to anyone with eyes, we stand at the cusp of global catastrophe. From ascending violence and chaos, to rising environmental crises, to growing psychological anguish and despair, the world is in dire straits and it is money that has

---

[13] The term "disconnection" is a term I use to refer, in lay terms, to a spiritual disconnection from "higher" consciousness. For details see the http://spiritwiki.lightningpath.org/Disconnection.

brought us to this point. We can still save the planet and ourselves, but we have to open our eyes to the crises, and we have to act fast. The first step to solving the crises was learning about the true nature of money. And now we have done that. The next step is learning about the problems with money and why money, for all its amazing and wonderful potential, has brought us to such an obvious and definitive brink.

THE PROBLEM WITH MONEY

As noted in the previous section, there are many benefits to a monetized economy; however, there are also potential problems. Some of the problems associated with money, like for example determining the monetary cost of a product, or motivating people to work, are minor and traceable. However other problems, like the problem of **accumulation**, are world ending problems. As we shall shortly see, accumulation causes massive distortions in human nature and human activity, and massive failures in the general economic fabric of life on this little global community we call Earth. Accumulation is bad, and that is the bottom line. In fact, when accumulation enters the equation, the world is set on a course of inevitable, world ending destruction. And by "world ending," I literally mean "world ending." The dynamic that is set up by the initiation of accumulation leads, if left unchecked, to the inevitable end of human civilization. Eventually the drive to accumulate destroys the environment, exalts inequality and injustice, and drives anger and desperation to critical levels. The result is the end of the world (as we know it). It might take a few thousand years, but the ugly end is destined from the naïve and innocent beginning. This is a strong statement I know, but perhaps you will see my point when you learn a little bit more about accumulation.

So, just what is accumulation?

Well, accumulation refers to the practice of accumulating labor power. In concrete terms, accumulation is the practice of taking somebody's labor and putting it on the shelf in your house. Simple! There is nothing wrong with that. We all do that. When I went to South Africa with my family, we bought many handicrafts from roadside artisans. We exchanged our money for their labor (i.e. the handicraft that they had created), and then we put their labor on the shelves and walls of our house. Although the artifacts in our home look like artistic objects, really what we have done is accumulate labor. The South African artisans put so many labor hours into the production of their craft, and now we have those labor hours objectified on our bookshelf at home. Again, there is nothing wrong with this, as long as the exchange was fair. It is nice to surround yourself with fine works of art and handicrafts, and it helps the artist and his or her family to eat.

Of course, some things are easier to accumulate than other things; similarly, some things are impossible to accumulate. Even though my wife exchanges money for a back massage, she cannot accumulate the massages she gets. In addition, there are practical limits on the accumulation of most things. My house can only contain so many elephant carvings and tribal masks before it starts to look cluttered, and I have to buy storage.

The difficulty of accumulating labor in the form of commodities and services generally makes accumulation a non-issue in societies based on barter. In barter-based economies, you work for what you need, accumulate a few things to make your life more pleasant, and it does not go much farther than that. In a barter-based economy there is a built-in limitation on accumulation. There really is no point in accumulating bread, hammers, computers, or handicrafts beyond a certain point because beyond a certain point, it looks and feels absurd.

Unfortunately, in a **monetized economy** it is a different story. In a monetized economy, there is no built-in limit to accumulation. In fact, in a monetized economy, you can accumulate as much labor power as you want. You can print a thousand-dollar bill, a million-dollar bill, a billion-dollar bill, and put it in the bank. It just does not matter; there is no limit. Since the value of money (i.e. the amount of labor it represents) is symbolic and based on a simple act of agreement rather than a reciprocal exchange of goods, you can accumulate as much labor (i.e. money) as you want. And that's a problem because the unlimited nature of accumulation can distort economies, invert economic purpose, and turn the entire economic system on its head.

And, it doesn't take that long to happen.

Remember what I said in the last section? An economy is a fundamentally social thing. Exchanging money is an act of social exchange. When I exchange my labor for your labor we are engaged in a social exchange. Money abstracts the social exchange just like money abstracts the value of the exchange, thereby making it harder to perceive; but the social nature of the exchange still exists. Unless of course it doesn't. In an accumulation economy you can totally write the social nature of the exchange out of the economic question. In an accumulation economy you can make accumulation (read profit) rather than social exchange of goods and services the primary economic goal. In its most absurd manifestation, accumulation becomes the entire point of doing business! As the former CEO of U.S. Steel famously said, "U.S. Steel is in the business to make profits (i.e. accumulate labor), not to make steel."[14]

In the context of comments about the fundamentally social nature of economic exchange, you can see just how twisted and perverse the CEO's statements are. His comments represent a total abdication of social purpose and a total corruption of economic activity. In the context of an accurate understanding of money as an efficient instrument for social/economic exchange, it makes no sense at all. In fact, the only way you can make it make any sense is to obfuscate the nature of money so that the social nature of the exchange and the reality of labor accumulation is obscured. If you obfuscate the nature of the exchange, then it becomes easier to stomach the business of profit. If the CEO of U.S. Steel said, "we are in the business of accumulating your labor," or "we don't care about the social fabric or the economy, we just want to take your labor power," you might be a little offended. However, when the CEO euphemizes the practice and says "we exist only to make money" it doesn't sound so bad. Money is just paper you use to buy things right? So what's wrong with "making money" after all?

In a monetized economy that has been corrupted to the point where accumulating labor power becomes the

---

[14] David McNally, "Power, Resistance, and the Global Economic Crisis," in *Power and Resistance: Critical Thinking About Canadian Social Issues*, ed. Les Samuelson and Wayne Antony(Halifax: Fernwood Publishing, 2012), 129. Parenthetical expression added.

primary goal of economic exchange, accumulation of labor power is euphemized as "profit" or "making money."

PROFIT

The obvious question at this point is, why would you want to do something as silly as make accumulation of labor (i.e., make "profit") the reason of your existence? In order to understand why you would want to make accumulation of labor the entire point of your existence, you have to understand something about the nature and possibilities inherent in accumulated labor power. The best way to understand that is with a story that I like to call the **Baker's Story**.

Let us start our story by imagining a few hundred people working in a small monetized economy, exchanging the fruits of their labor. Life is great and everybody is happily working away their days doing things that they love to do, and exchanging their labor fairly. Now imagine that one day, sometime after the monetization of our small economy, somebody gets the idea to charge just a little bit more for their labor than is strictly fair. Let us say that this person is the baker, whom we will call Joe. Let us imagine that instead of charging say .50 labor units for each loaf of bread, the actual cost of the bread,[15] Joe now starts to charge

---

[15] To determine the labor cost of the bread, the baker divides the total labor time it takes to make the bread by the number of loaves made. For example, if the baker bakes nine loaves of bread in three hours including clean up, the labor value of a loaf of his bread is three divided by 9 or .33 labor units. If he adds the cost of his flour, oil, and yeast (all of which have their own labor

27

.66 units (twice the real cost), .99 units (three times the real cost), or whatever. Joe surmises that it is not much really, and it does not seem like it is going to hurt anything or anyone, so what is the harm with accumulating a little extra labor? "What's the problem with taking a little 'profit' for oneself?" he asks.

As it turns out, it is a big problem. In fact, as noted, it is a world-ending problem; however, that is not immediately apparent when the machine is just starting up. It takes a while to show up, so let us skip ahead and take a look at Joe a year later to see what has happened with his plan to accumulate labor. It is not difficult to imagine. After a year of charging more than the true labor value of his bread, Joe will have accumulated a bunch of extra labor. How much extra labor will Joe have accumulated? Well, if he charges three times the actual labor cost for his bread, at the end of the year he is going to have accumulated twice as much labor as he actually put into his business. If a typical person expends 1,500 units a year, then Joe, having charged everybody triple the cost of the bread, will be in the black by some 3,000 labor units. Everybody else's balance sheet is close to zero, but even after a single year of "profitable" operation, Joe is way ahead of the pack.

POWER

You have to admit, accumulating a little extra labor sounds very cool, especially if your name is Joe. It is even cooler when you realize what you can do with all that accumulated

---

value), it might raise the cost of the bread to.50 units per bread loaf.

labor, and it is not rocket science. Take a good look at that dollar bill in your wallet. Remember the nature of money. Money is a container for labor. When it is accumulated, money has the ability to command (i.e. buy) other people's labor. Pause and think about this for a moment, because this extra money, this *accumulated labor,* gives Joe the baker an incredible amount of real, palpable, and measurable **power**. Really, the possibilities are endless for our newly wealthy baker man. With the extra 3,000 units of labor, he can do whatever he wants whenever he wants because he can command other people to work for him. He can hire staff and take an extended vacation, he can have a bigger house made for himself, and he can employ a house cleaner to clean his home.

And how cool is that?

Since the money in his pocket represents abstract labor time, as long as he can find someone willing to work for the cash, Joe can do whatever he wants. With extra labor units to command he can now have more and do more than anybody else. He now has power that others do not.[16]

---

[16] Interestingly enough, power does not necessarily enter into monetary relationships. Assuming equality of conditions (i.e. I have all the money I need and you have all the money you need), power cannot enter the equation. If I have all the money I need, and you ask me to do something I do not want to do, I do not have to do it because I have enough money. However, if for some reason I need your money, if I am unemployed, if I am broke, if my bank account is drained by interest, if I need to feed and protect my kids, or keep a roof over my head, and you control the money, then you have the power. If you ask me to do something, because I need the money you have, I will often do

"It's brilliant," thinks Joe when he pauses at year-end accounting to consider the benefits and ethics of it all. He looks up from his books, he looks around at the world, and he realizes, he is now a bit different from everybody else around him. Because he thought to charge a little extra for his bread, at the end of a year, he now has power and capability that no one else has.

"But is that wrong?" he asks himself.

"Nobody seems to have gotten hurt," he says to himself, "and nothing seems to have changed in the wider society."

"So what's the harm?" he decides.

"Really" he thinks to himself, "the only problem that I have now is how to use this extra labor power." Joe thinks about it and after some consideration, he decides to spend the extra labor units he has accumulated on a beautiful mansion, twice the size of all the other houses around him. He builds his beautiful mansion on the top of a local hill overlooking his little community. Of course, it is not something he could have done a year earlier. Before he

---

things I would not even think of doing if I did not *need* the money. Think about the job you are doing now. Do you love what you do? If not, why do you do it? If you had enough money to do what you wanted to do, would you do the current job? If not, what would you do instead? It is an awesome question to ask because it gives you an indication of what life would be like in a properly monetized economy. If an economy is properly monetized (i.e. if money hasn't been greedily extracted to the point where there is not enough money to go around), a lot of jobs that people currently do would no longer exist because we wouldn't be forced to do them. This is something to keep in mind as we wind our way through this short economic essay.

started his little accumulation experiment, he would not have had the power to command all the labor required; but now he can! Joe has got all that extra cash so now he can build a beautiful mansion on the top of the hill; and that is what he does. And that is when his community starts to notice. That is when the questions start.

"Hey Mr. Baker Man, what the heck's going on?" ask his friends.

"Where did all your cash come from, and how did you manage to build that big house?" they ask him.

The questions stop him in his tracks. What is he going to do, and how is he going to answer? Is he going to come clean and reveal the (real) secret[17] to his success (i.e. that he is charging more for his bread than it is actually worth), or is he going to hide the truth so that he can keep accumulating labor? He thinks about coming clean but to be honest with himself, he does not like the implications. He figures if he comes clean, the jig is up and his free ride is over. After all, nobody in his community is going to stand by and let him overcharge for his bread. Not only that, he also suspects that his community will be a little pissed at him. Heck, they may even demand restitution. That would suck, thinks Baker Joe. Paying back 3,000 units of labor would mean he would have to sell his house or work triple

---

[17] Like the word "profit" is a euphemism for accumulation, the so-called Law of Attraction (LOA) is an obfuscation of the real dynamic of accumulation as well. That is, the "secret" to prosperity isn't some magical, wishful thinking, the secret to prosperity is to accumulate another person's labor power. That's the real secret, and it is a secret that the LOA pundits help obscure when they babble about attraction.

time over the next year just to rebalance the financial sheets; and he doesn't want to do that. Besides, despite their questions, no harm has come from it. He has a little more than everybody else does, but that is not so bad. Despite some minor grumbling, everybody is still working, and everybody is still happy.

"So what if I've got a bigger house than everybody else?" he asks himself.

"Where is the harm in that?"

A PRIVATE PARTY

So, what does Joe do?

Well, he can't do nothing. Everybody in his community is asking questions and he has to respond to them. However, instead of issuing a public announcement like he should, instead of taking the time to talk to everybody at once, instead of revealing the real secret to his success, in other words, instead of doing the right thing, he tells his community he'd rather talk to only a few people at first.

"It's complicated and hard to explain," he says to his fellow community members, "so if you don't mind it will be easier if I talk to a few people at first. After I have explained it to them, they can report to you."

Of course, nobody sees a problem with this. Members of the community have always trusted each other and so if Joe says it is complicated and he needs some space to explain, it must be true. After all, why would Joe lie?

Joe says he needs to talk to a few people first, so that is what he does. One night he invites a few carefully chosen people over. He invites the carpenter (whom he paid extra to build his house) and a few of his closest friends over for a sumptuous and luxurious dinner. He spares no expense. He takes a thousand accumulated labor units and he hires an army to throw a party like no party that has ever been thrown before. Because he can command all that extra labor, the party is impressive and magnificent. When it is over, Joe and his friends sit down to the finest cognac. There is idle chitchat while Joe patiently waits for the warm cognac glow to spread through the body and mind of each of his guests. When he is sure their hearts have been warmed by the cognac, Joe stands up and offers a toast.

"My dear friends," he exclaims, "it has been a wonderful meal, impeccable company, and I am happier than I have ever been in my life."

Everybody at the table nods in enthusiastic agreement.

"It is an honor and a privilege to share these blessings with you tonight," he says, "but now," he says as he nods with serious intent "we should get down to business."

My dear friends," he says, "if I could tell you how you could have a mansion like mine..."

"...if I could show you how to make every night a night like this," he pauses.

"...would you be interested?"

His friends look at each other with excitement. "Of course," they say, "that is why we are here."

"Yes," Joe says nodding in agreement, "and I will tell you."

"But you know," says Joe quietly with his head bowed down and his eyes looking intently up at his guests, "this only works if you keep it a secret!"

At this statement, a palpable shock wave goes through the room. There is a buzz of discussion and puzzled looks. The people sitting in the room have never been asked to keep a secret like this before, so they are justifiably wary and concerned. They start to raise their concerns and formulate their questions, but Joe raises his hand to silence them, smiles, pours more cognac into their glasses, and assures them there is nothing to worry about.

"Nobody gets harmed," he says. "In fact, everybody wins!" he exclaims as he nods his head enthusiastically. "And I can prove it to you, but it took me a year to figure it out, so it is going to take you a year as well."

"Try it for a year," he says, "and when the year is over you will understand."

"Can everyone do that?" he asks.

Joe makes sure to keep the glasses full as his friends discuss the issue. They raise some relatively minor objections, which Joe easily counters because they don't really have a clue what he's doing, and by the end of their discussion none of them can see what the harm could possibly be.

"The baker is right," they say. "Only good things have come from this. Who wouldn't want to have parties like this all the time?" So, agreeing to keep the secret for a year, they shake hands, toast Joe, congratulate themselves and their wisdom and wit, and confidently sit down to plan. They will try it for a year and then decide what to do after that. Nobody is worried; everybody trusts Joe. He is their friend and he has assured them it is a win-win situation.

THE TRUTH?

To the people on top of the hill, the decision to keep the truth a secret for a year so they would all have time to learn Joe's "secret" seemed like a good plan. The only problem was, the people at the bottom of the hill were expecting a report from those who went to the party. This was a problem for the people at the top. What were they going to say? They already agreed amongst themselves that they would keep silent; but they could not just say to the people at the bottom, "Tough luck, we're going to keep it a secret." If the people at the top told the truth that they were keeping it all a secret, the people at the bottom would get angry; that would be no good. Everybody at the top agreed, this was a problem that could not be ignored. But what were they going to do? They consider the problem for quite some time until finally the carpenter who had built the mansion

35

jumped up and exclaimed excitedly, "I know, I know, I know!!! We'll tell them the truth!"

There were puzzled looks from his top-of-the-hill colleagues.

"We'll say we need to study the problem!" he says.

His colleagues crinkle their eyebrows in confusion.

"We'll say the issue is complicated, that we don't fully understand, that we need to do some research, and therefore we need more time to look!"

"And it's true, isn't it?", asks the carpenter.

"Isn't this exactly what we are doing!" he says, unable to contain his excitement.

Of course, everyone agrees. Research is exactly what they are doing; so, they jot down some notes, pick their best public speaker, set a date, and call the people at the bottom together. When the day comes, it is very exciting for the people at the bottom because everybody expects to learn the wonderful secret to Joe's wealth. Indeed, everybody is anticipating great prosperity and so all the people and all their children congregate in the town square, excited by what is about to be announced.

They gather round and look up.

The speaker enters from the left.

He climbs the podium and looks down and out over the gathered crowd.

He smiles and says with a monotone drone, "People of our community, listen to me. Joe, our esteemed baker, has stumbled upon the secret to great prosperity."

The speaker nods slowly, gazing across the crowd.

"Indeed," he nods, smiling a crooked smile, "The baker has found a way to make money."

A hush falls over the crowd.

"Unfortunately," says the speaker, "it is complicated and not well understood."

"We have been studying the discovery and we tentatively may conclude that it is a combination of the relative fluctuation of commodity indexes, plus the increase in constant pricing of goods and services on the market exchange, over and above the cost of the inputs as opposed to outputs."

His monotone intonation and complicated verbiage bores and confuses.

He continues, "It is the result of the de-indexing of commodity pricing in relation to the cost of inputs and labor."

The crowd looks baffled.

Sensing the crowd's confusion, the speaker solemnly nods his head in agreement.

"Yes," he says, his chin wagging up and down, "it is complicated."

"But," he says thumping his chest, "we shall not rest until we figure it out."

"We shall work day and night."

"We shall pursue the truth and we shall persevere until we find it."

He nods and smiles a self-satisfied little grin.

"In order to assist with the process," he says, "we have started an institute that we will call **The Institute of Fiduciary Investigation**, or just **The Institute** for short."

"For the good of the community we shall labor day and night until we discover the inner essence of this complicated process. When we understand, we shall share with you so that you too can benefit from the baker's great wisdom. We shall report to you in exactly one year," he says, abruptly raising his hands to avoid the emerging questions. He turns, steps down off the podium, and walks quickly off of the stage.

Of course, there is a bit of confusion. Everybody was expecting an explanation, but they didn't get that. All they got was confusion, EPMO,[18] and a promise of future revelations. Still, what the speaker had said seemed reasonable enough. They had all heard the speaker try to 39explain things, and it certainly did sound complicated.

---

[18] **EPMO** (pronounced ep-mo) is shorthand for the phrase **Egotistical, Polly-syllabic, Multi-metaphoric, Obfuscation**. This phrase is used to describe, in a tongue-in-cheek fashion, the tortuous correspondences, arbitrary associations, and toxic grammatical complexity used by some writers to obscure truth, divert attention, hide their own ignorance, or bolster their own ego. EPMO is common in esoteric spiritual and scientific writing, but can be found anywhere ideology, ignorance, and ego abound. See http://spiritwiki.lightningpath.org/EPMO.

Everybody in the community trusted each other and so the people at the bottom of the hill had no reason to question what the speaker had said. Why not be patient and wait, they thought. They accepted the explanation in good faith and they all went home to patiently, and quietly, wait for the report.

In the meantime, the people who had been at Joe's special party gradually started, at the behest of the baker man, to raise their prices over and above the actual cost of their labor in order so that they too could generate some "profit."

And thus did the end begin.

THE FALL

Of course, as soon as the boys from the top of the hill started to raise their prices, the inevitable happened. After only a year of subtle accumulation, all the people from the party had built fancy houses on top of the hill right alongside their baker friend.

"Isn't this great," they said to themselves at one of their now weekly (and increasingly secret) meetings.

"Joe was right," they said, smiling. "Look at what we've accomplished; and, nobody has gotten hurt! Despite the fact that we have all moved up the hill and are now living in fancy houses, eating fine food, and drinking fine wine, the economy is working and nothing untoward seems to have happened."

"What a wonderful world this truly is," they say, convinced that nothing is wrong. But then again, they are in active self-delusion. They can clearly see that something important has changed; they are just blithely ignoring it. Instead of everyone being equal members of an equal society,  exchanging labor in a fair and equitable arrangement, some people are different. Now, society is divided into two distinct "classes" of people, each with different interests and different lifestyles. The dividing lines are obvious. There are the families at the top of the hill with their big houses and their lavish parties, and there are the families at the bottom who live a more modest existence. The new class nature of the society caused by the secret accumulation of those at the top is obvious; but, it hardly seems significant, at least to the people at the top of the hill.

"What's the big deal anyway," they say to themselves, "and why even think about it?"

"Isn't this the way it should always have been," they say?

"And doesn't God want it this way?"

"And isn't this part of nature's evolutionary plan?"

"And besides," say the people at the top, "everybody is happy with what they have got!"

"It is all right, and proper, and true," they tell themselves over and over and over again. But really, how would they know? By the end of the second year, the people at the top of the hill no longer socialize with the people at the bottom of the hill. The people at the top have their own private meetings, their own private functions, and the two groups just don't fit together anymore. It is mostly a question of income and comfort. The people at the bottom of the hill simply cannot keep up with the lavish extravagance of the people at the top of the hill. Compared to their former friends at the top of the hill, they are poor and they feel uncomfortable and inadequate being around the extravagance. If truth be told, they are not altogether happy about that. Indeed, they are starting to get a little grumpy. All those fancy houses and extravagant parties are a constant reminder that even two years on, they still haven't

41

received any answers. All they have is a promise; all they see is the rapid emergence of **social class.**[19]

"That's not right," say the increasingly angry and agitated people at the bottom of the hill.

They furrow their brows, they wring out their hands, and they growl "What happened at that first party, and what is going on?"

They ask their questions, but they get no answers and their anger and agitation grows. The speaker reappears from time to time reassuring the people at the bottom that the people at the top are still studying the problem, but because he really does nothing but divert, eventually his appearance just makes the people even angrier. Time passes, frustration grows, and discontent and displeasure ascend in a rising crescendo of menace (to the people at the top). Pitchforks and pokey things start finding their way into the hands of the people at the bottom, and that makes Joe and his buddies quite uncomfortable. They know they have to do something otherwise bad things are going to start happening. They hold a special emergency meeting at which they decide it is time for The Institute to release a special report. The people at the top tell the people at The Institute to pen the report and release it *tout de suite.* They give the people at The Institute some "special instructions" on how to write the report and before you know it, and just in time, the report is in the hands of the people at the bottom of the hill.

---

[19] http://spiritwiki.lightningpath.org/Social_Class.

THE REPORT

Sadly, but not unexpectedly, when the report is finally released, there is no satisfaction to be found. The problem is that nobody can understand it. The report is so full of jargon, gobbledygook, and EPMO that it is a thousand times more confusing than the original speech was. By the tenth page just about everybody reading it is either confused or asleep. Those who are confused are too embarrassed to ask questions, and those who are asleep obviously cannot. This is great for the people at the top of the hill because now the people at the bottom are too embarrassed thinking that they might just be too stupid to understand, or too confused and turned around, to ask any questions. Not wanting to leave it at this however, the people at the top go a step further. Inserted at the beginning of the report is a one-page executive summary that everybody can understand. This summary sends a clear and clarion message to the people at the bottom of the hill. "The problem is multifaceted, the situation is complex, and the variables are indeterminate. More time will be needed to study."

INTELLIGENTSIA

Now, if you are one of those people at the bottom of the hill reading the report and hoping for satisfaction, you would likely find it hard to hide your disappointment, confusion, and anger. After all, a couple of years have passed and the only thing that seems to be happening is that the people at the top of the hill are getting richer, more extravagant, and more lavish all the time. Frankly, it is a little hard to stomach. Still, most people at the bottom of the hill face the situation and go back to work. After all, they trust the people at *The Institute*; when they say they are working on the problem, they must be working on the problem. Still, a few of the people at the bottom of the hill do not give in to the pressure to feel stupid, do not feel embarrassed by their lack of understanding, and do not go calmly back to work. A few are unhappy about the whole thing and they frown, grumble, complain, and continue to ask difficult questions.

"What's going on?" they ask, "And why is it taking so long?"

"Why are there so many new mansions being built?"

"Why can't we get a straight answer?"

Of course, all these questions make the families at the top of the hill a little nervous. If these agitators keep complaining, they will eventually get the other people angry again. Clearly, the people at the top of the hill can't just let the agitators keep agitating. Something has to be done. So, the people call a special meeting of their now very exclusive and very secret boys' club to discuss the problem. As usual, after a butler serves a dinner of fine wine and food, the elected chairman stands and says...

"Most honorable and dignified gentlemen of the innermost circle of Illuminated Back Scratchers International (I-BS-I) society, we have a problem."

"As you know, the report did not provide satisfaction or clarity."

"The problem is multifaceted," he says echoing the conclusions of the report and believing his own BS.

"The situations are complex; the variables indeterminate," he says. "Obviously, more study is needed."

"Unfortunately," he muses, "some people from the bottom of the hill do not seem to understand this. They are asking the same old questions, and agitating the people for answers. Their discontent grows stronger every day. And who knows where that might lead..." his voice trails off.

"But what can we do?" he asks.

"Until The Institute reaches a point of clarity, there are no answers and there can be no satisfaction."

"Therefore," says the chairman, "I have a proposal that may be a possible solution."

"Those agitators..." he says pausing for effect.

"The ones who aren't satisfied with the report..." he continues.

"The ones asking all those uncomfortable questions and getting everybody agitated as a result..."

"I believe," says he, "that they are simply a little smarter than everyone else."

He nods and smiles.

"And you know," he says as his eyes scan the faces of the gathered dignitaries, "we could *use* people like that to help out at The Institute! We could use their brain power and hopefully, with a little 'direction from above', they can help bring clarity" he says, smiling a broad but crooked smile.

"We can bring them into the fold, show them how difficult it is, and maybe then they will stop their agitation."

He looks around the room at the surprised faces but of course, after a few moments thought, everyone agrees that it is a brilliant idea. The agitators want answers, so why not co-opt them and put them into a position where it is their responsibility to provide them.

"It will satisfy the agitators," says the chairman, "*and* it will remove their influence from the bottom of the hill."

"The only problem," he says, "is how will we get them to The Institute?"

"Why would they add their voice to something they already see as problematic?" wonders the chairman out loud.

But, he has an answer for that. "We'll do what we always do," he says, "We'll just tell them the truth!"

"We'll tell them that we need their help."

"We'll tell them that we haven't been able to bring clarity."

"We'll tell them we're just a bunch of dim-witted business people and we need their intellectual prowess to save the day."

"How can they say no to that?" asks the chairman. "And, just to sweeten the deal, we'll give them a small bonus. We'll pay them a little more than the people at the bottom! We'll give them a taste of what it's like," said Joe. "Not too much though! We do not want them as neighbors at the top of the hill," he says. "After all, it is already too crowded at the top. But, there is lots of space in the middle," he says cheerfully, "so we'll help them get set up down there. It is an offer they won't be able to refuse," concludes the chairman, nodding his head and removing the cotton from between his cheeks.

46

And so the letters of invitation go out, bonuses are offered, and the agitators and their families pack up their bags, stroke their own egos, and begin the short trek up to employment at The Institute, and life at the middle of the hill.

INDOCTRINATION

When the new intelligentsia arrive at The Institute, there is a magnificent ceremony of welcome. There is fine wine, gourmet food, and a charismatic keynote speaker hired to address the newcomers and set the tone for the work they will carry out. When everybody has filled their bellies with fine wine and food, the speaker climbs the podium and says to the assembled guests...

"Honored guests... Thank you for coming."

"Thank you for accepting our invitation."

"Thank you for agreeing to help us."

"For two years we have struggled," says the speaker.

"For two years we have labored into the night."

"We have collected data, we have poured over charts, we have analyzed patterns, but still we lack clarity," she says shaking her head.

"But now we are hopeful," she says smiling broadly and raising her hands towards the audience, "because now *you* are here. We are confident that with your help we will bring clarity. With your fine minds, and your deep motivation for truth, we will succeed!" she declares.

"But first," says the speaker, "there must be a period of study."

"You must understand the issues."

"A couple of years are all it will require." She raises her hands to fend off the questions that start to percolate through the assembled guests.

"It is necessary," nods the speaker. "We have labored for two years and in that time we have made much progress. We have developed new ideas and discovered new concepts, and these ideas and concepts inform our studies and help us communicate our findings."

"But," she says, "there are many new concepts and it is a complicated language. Before you can help us you must learn to speak that language."

"I am sure you will all agree," she says, "there is no sense in reinventing the wheel."

And of course, the honored guests agree. Why would they not? After all, they might be a little unhappy with the performance of The Institute, but that is what they are there to help with. Beyond that, they trust the good faith of their colleagues and agree that it will be most efficient if they build on what has gone before. Sadly, they do not question the motivation of the people who brought them up the hill. Therefore, they will enter a period of study where they will learn the language and the concepts used at The Institute. With the decision made, they finish their meal, drink their wine, and shuffle off to bed in order that they will be bright and fresh for their very first day of indoctrination, err, study, in the morning.

EDUCATION

When the new employees of The Institute wake up the next day, they begin to study. The day after that, they study as well. The day after that, they study again. For two years they study and in that time they learn how to think and talk just like The Institute founders. When their superiors are satisfied that the agitators will think, talk, and act just like them, they set the new "professionals" to work collecting data, pouring over charts, and analyzing patterns. They work hard and they work long. But unfortunately, no matter how much work the former agitators do, at the end of each day they still lack clarity.

Something is always missing.

Something just doesn't fit.

Still, they work diligently within the conceptual rubric *provided* by The Institute; and, every once in a while they issue a report. Obviously, since the newcomers have learned to think, talk, and act just like the founders of The Institute, the report always says the same thing. Amid all the specialized jargon, technical concepts, and economic "hoax us, poke us" that seems to get more complicated every year (and which nobody at the bottom of the hill can ever understand), the report always says...

It is complicated and more study is needed.

And of course, every time the people at the bottom of the hill hear that, they are very disappointed; but what can they do? The people at the bottom of the hill know that the best minds they have to offer are working on the problem. They believe that if anybody can do it, they can do it. So, they bury their disappointment, trust their comrades, and go back to work while the people at the top continue to accumulate.

It seems like a good system and largely it works, in the interests of the people at the top of the hill at least. Of course, there are problems. Each year when the report is released there are always a few people who cannot hide their disappointment. They gripe, grumble, and agitate and the people at the top always worry where it might go. To solve this problem, the people at the top of the hill scout the people at the bottom. They identify the agitators and invite them to work at The Institute. The agitators invariably accept the offer and move to the middle of the hill. There they are indoctrinated (err, educated) and released into the laboratory where they labor with their comrades and release their yearly reports which always and invariably say the same thing.

It is complicated and more study is needed.

And so it goes that the people at the bottom are fooled again and again and again.

TAXATION

You have to admit, it was/is a perfect system and it worked brilliantly for a long time until one day The Institute grew too big and the financial strain on the people at the top became too much. Too many employees meant a huge labor bill, and the people at the top simply could not pay for it by themselves, at least not without affecting their standard of living. In order to deal with the growing bill, the Grand Poohbah Baker Joe calls a special meeting.

"Most illustrious and honored brothers," he says, "I call you here today because of a problem that is emerging. Up until now we have, as a benefit to the people and out of the kindness of our hearts, funded The Institute."

"It has all been out of our own pockets," he says with voice rising, "and that has worked!

"But The Institute is growing and its costs are increasing."

"We can no longer afford this kindness on our own."

"Of course," he says laughing, "getting rid of The Institute or scaling back operations is not yet an option. Not only does The Institute provide us with invaluable yearly reports that mollify the population, it also provides a great place to put people who aren't happy living at the bottom."

"Still," says Joe, "something must be done to relieve us of the cost while ensuring The Institute continues to perform."

He looks around at the anxious faces, nervous smiles, and says "Don't worry! I believe I have a solution. We shall get the people at the bottom of the hill to pay for it," he says, smiling broadly.

"After all, The Institute primarily serves them, does it not?"

"We," he says, spreading his arms to encompass the wealth that surrounds them all, "do not need The Institute."

"We," he says with an expansive and knowing grin on his face, "do not need the answers."

"The Institute is for them," he says as he points down the hill. "They asked for the answers, not us; therefore, it is only fair that they should pay!"

"As always," smiles the baker, "we'll just tell them the truth. They need it more than we do so they should be expected to pay."

Upon hearing his explanation, everyone agrees. So, they hire the best public speaker money can buy and call an assembly of the people at the bottom of the hill. The speaker climbs the podium and speaks...

"These are times of great potential," he intones.

"These are times of great promise," his head nods up and down.

"Look at what is possible with industry and fortitude," he says, pointing to the mansions at the top of the hill.

"Look at what hard work can bring."

"But there is no need to thank us", the speaker says as he raises his hands as if pushing someone away.

"We do this not for gratitude or prestige, we do this because you are our brothers and sisters."

"We care for you and we have always wanted to help."

"But," he says, "we can no longer do it alone."

"Each year The Institute has grown and each year the cost becomes more onerous."

"We need your help," he says reaching out his palms to the people.

"It won't be much."

"Just a few pennies a week."

"You'll barely feel it," he says.

"And if you want," says the speaker, his voice becoming shrill and annoying, "you can always make it up by working just a little bit harder."

He smiles and looks around.

He sees the people beneath him talking and for a moment there is some doubt....

Maybe they will not believe him this time...

But finally the people begin to smile and nod.

He sighs relief because he can see that everybody at the bottom of the hill agrees.

"Why would they not," he says to himself.

They are good people, he scoffs.

"God's people," he sneers.

And they always will believe what we tell them.

They will always have faith in their brothers and sisters.

And so he speaks again.

"You are good people," he says, "God's people!" he says, "and I am proud of you."

"You believe what we say and you trust your brothers and sisters."

"We have asked for your help and you have given it to us, for you see that we are only here to serve."

"And we thank you for that," he says as he turns and steps down off the stage, anxious to get back to his yacht.

And so the people at the bottom work just a little harder to pay for the new taxes being used to fund the Institute.

"But that's OK," they tell themselves.

"We are good people," they say.

"We are God's people," they cry, "and we must always do our fair share."

And with their "nose to the grindstone," and with their blood, sweat, and tears, they do.

And every year The Institute releases a new report.

And every year it says the same thing, (i.e. it is complicated and more study is needed).

And every year there are new agitators.

But, every year the agitators are co-opted.

At first it is economics, a discipline designed to help understand the economy. Then it is engineering, a discipline designed to increase production expertise. Then it is philosophy, a discipline designed to help understand why the "natural" way the world is divided between those at the top, and those at the bottom. Then it is history, a discipline designed to tell the story from the perspective of those at the top of the hill. Then it is psychology, to control the workers and keep them docile. Finally, it is sociology, a discipline that provides valuable insight on the actions and motivations of the people at the bottom of the hill. Pretty soon, The Institute is everywhere, which is great because with The Institute operating to manage discontent and provide obscure explanations, everything is working fantastically. And, with everything working so well, the boys at the top of the hill now have time to deal with other issues besides system maintenance and so, finally, they turn their full attention to the thing they love the most.

And so it goes that the people at the bottom are fooled again and again and again.

PROGRESS

Of course, the people at the top are not content to just sit back and enjoy. They love the power that accumulation brings and they always want more. It is a great time for them. With things working so well, The Institute functioning smoothly, and the masses footing the bill, people at the top could now turn their full attention to the thing they loved the best—accumulation! One day after a particularly lavish dinner, Joe the baker stands and speaks.

"Didn't I tell you it would be this way?" he says raising his glass for a toast.

"Didn't I say?"

"Nobody has been harmed," he smiles with great satisfaction.

"In fact," says Joe, "quite the opposite has occurred."

"Look around you at the changes we have brought!"

"We the people at the top have created a better world!" he exclaims dramatically.

"Our homes are the pinnacle of architectural innovation and our gardens are the summit of creativity and beauty."

"And The Institute," he says, "is our crowning glory."

"Congratulations to all of us," Joe says raising his glass and toasting the room.

"We the people have brought progress to this world."

He pauses for a moment and then begins to speak slowly.

"But," says Joe, "we can do more."

"We can improve everything."

"We can lead this world to utopia."

"Indeed, with the proper preparation, we could bring a new world order that would increase our wealth and prosperity a billion fold."

"All we need," he says, "is more money so we can do it."

PRODUCT DIFFERENTIATION

"And I know just how to get it," Joe says.

"I know how we can fund utopia."

"All we have to do is increase the rate of extraction and storage of labor, and I have found multiple ways to do that," he says triumphantly.

"Instead of making only one kind of bread," he says, "instead of making only the finest bread that I am capable of making, I can make a cheaper bread with cheaper ingredients and less care. I can sell that cheaper bread to the people at the bottom of the hill."

"If I do this," he says, "I will save money on ingredients and labor and therefore I will accumulate more."

He looks around the room at the attentive, smiling faces.

"There's more," he continues. "I can also make special bread with the finest ingredients and the most care and attention and I can sell that special bread to the people higher up the hill for a premium. Instead of three times the cost, I can sell the premium bread for five times the cost, or even ten."

"And yes," he says anticipating their questions, "they will buy it. All I have to do is tell them this bread is only for the 'special' ones, and in order to feel special, they will buy it."

"But," says the baker, "there is a slight problem. When the people at the bottom of the hill come into the shop and find they can afford only the cheap bread, they will probably grumble and complain."

"Of course," says the baker gravely, "we all know where that leads."

"But," says Joe smiling, "I have learned that in order to curtail their grumbling I simply need to tell them the truth. When they complain I will tell them, 'This is the price that you have to pay for progress,' and that will quiet them down because nobody can argue with progress."

"And further," says the baker, "I'll tell them it is all in their hands and it is always their fault anyway!"

"If they work a little harder..."

"If they stay a little longer ..."

"If they save their money..."

"Then they too will be able to afford the special bread."

The baker looks around the room, smiling.

"In the name of progress?" he asks raising his glass.

"In the name of progress!" cry his brothers as they toast the baker and quaff their wine.

DISTORTION

And so it goes. In the name of progress, the people at the top of the hill begin to look for ways to increase their rate of accumulation. They do not stop with product differentiation. After all, the goal is "progress" (i.e. more accumulation) and the more efficient they can make accumulation, the more progress there will be. So, each week they meet with one another and share their ideas for more efficient accumulation.

One week they come up with *planned obsolescence* and *product lifecycle.* Instead of designing products to last, those who can get away with it design products to break or go out of fashion after some time has passed. In this way, they ensure that *consumers,* as the people at the bottom of the hill have come to be known, are tied into perpetual product purchase. Of course, planned obsolescence and product lifecycle[20] means the people at the bottom of the hill have to work harder and longer in order to fund The Institute, buy the special bread, replace worn-out products, and afford each year's new fashions; but, as the people at the top say, "that's the price you pay." Of course, and

---

[20] Planned obsolescence and product life cycle has pinnacled, with horrendous psychological, emotional, and environmental consequences in what has become known as **Fast Fashion**. It is no understatement to say that the fast fashion industry is single handedly contributing to massive suffering and destruction.

There is lots of information online about this horrific development. See for example Shannon Whitehead, "5 Truths the Fast Fashion Industry Doesn't Want You to Know," *Huff Post Style,* August 19 2014. An excellent documentary on the topic of fast fashion is Andrew Morgan, "The True Cost,"(2015).

unfortunately, obsolescence and product life cycle also means an expanding strain on the resources of Mother Earth as shoddy consumer goods and broken consumer products come to saturate the landfills and devour resources. "But these things," says Baker Joe, "are small prices to pay for progress."

And so "the band" plays on.

One week they come up with an idea to lower labor costs by paying people at the bottom of the hill less for the work they do. Of course, this is not a very popular idea among the people at the bottom because it requires them, their spouses, and sometimes even their children, to work harder and longer just to get by. However, the people at the top of the hill are persistent and in the name of "progress" they find ways to force the issue. They deskill labor,[21] tie the workers to assembly lines, keep demand for

---

[21] In this regard, have a look at Frederick Winslow Taylor. Taylor was an American mechanical engineer instrumental in the development of what became known as *Scientific Management.* His goal was to increase production and profits. He expended great effort rationalizing the factory floor, speeding up work, deskilling the workers, imposing surveillance and manipulating them emotionally. He was quite successful and has become a bit of a hero to industrialists the world over.

Wikipedia has a decent summary of Mr. Taylor and his work, but the best place for information and analysis comes from the sociologists studying work and industry in the labor process tradition. See for example David Knights and Hugh Willmott, *Labour Process Theory*(London: Macmillan Press, 1990). For Mr. Taylor's Wikipedia page, and for additional information on scientific management, Taylorism, etc., see

key professions lower by restricting access to education, and even use child labor in countries where they can get away with it. Of course, the people at the top recognize the unpleasant nature of these things; but "there is always a price to be paid for progress," they tell themselves.

And so, "the band" plays on.

One week, the people at the top notice that many people at the bottom of the hill are still using the informal economy to exchange labor by barter. They think about this and conclude that this is a bad thing because when people barter with each other, it is impossible to accumulate their labor. And, as the people at the top keep saying, when there is no accumulation, there is no progress. Therefore, in order to ensure ongoing and increasing accumulation, the people at the top of the hill decide that bartering should be reduced and eventually eliminated. Obviously, the people at the bottom resist. In their eyes, barter has always been a legitimate form of trade. To give it up would put them at a further disadvantage; but the people at the top of the hill are persistent and in the name of progress they eventually get their way. With the help of The Institute, they commission a report that says that activity outside of the main economy is detrimental to the progress of the nation. They then instruct the government to begin counting all forms of economic activity. Finally,

---

Wikipedia, "Frederick Winslow Taylor,"
https://en.wikipedia.org/wiki/Frederick_Winslow_Taylor.

they reorganize production. Instead of having small, locally self-sufficient economies where informal exchange and barter is easy and natural, they force a separation of production and make whole countries that specialize in single product lines. They grow bananas in one country, build cars in another, get grain  from a third, exploit Bangladeshi children to make clothes, and so on. It works brilliantly. In a globally dispersed marketplace where you get your food from farmers who live thousands of miles away, barter becomes impossible.

And so, "the band" plays on.

Each week, the men and women from the top of the hill meet to discuss how to bring "progress" to the world, and every once in a while someone comes up with a new and better way to grip and squeeze and slurp. Through all this, the people at the bottom of the hill work harder and harder just trying to keep up. "But that," say the people at the top of the hill, "is the price we pay for progress."

And so, the band plays on until one day a new problem begins to emerge, and the problem is money. As it turns out, all the effort that the people at the top of the hill are putting into developing efficient ways to create "progress" (i.e. accumulate more wealth) are creating an uncomfortably rapid flow of cash. The problem is, they have so much money it is collecting in filthy and moldy piles. It is ridiculous, not to mention ugly, dirty, and unsanitary. It is a problem for sure. Initially, the people at the top of the hill do not know what to do with all the money they are accumulating. They call a special meeting to discuss the problem. They talk and they talk and they eventually find a solution. To make a long story short, they find a better container for their money.

METAL AND ROCK

It is the stonemason who figures it out. One day at one of their special private meetings, the stonemason sheepishly raises his hand and says to the assembled brothers and sisters, "I think I might have a solution to our problem with money." He calls them into a circle and beckons them to look as he reaches into his pocket to pull out a beautiful gold ring with a huge shiny rock in it. He shows it around the room as he begins to explain, "About six months ago my cash flow was such that I no longer had to work for a living." He pauses while the members of the club raise their glasses and congratulate his hard work and good fortune.

63

"But I was bored," he says, "and I needed something to fill my time. Being a stonemason by trade, I started to play with rocks and metals and I discovered that these shiny rocks could be cut into these beautiful sparkly shapes. Further, I discovered that I could take this soft and shiny metal and bend it and shape it. Finally," says the stonemason as he raises the diamond ring in triumph, "I discovered that I could combine the two."

Everybody admires the rock in his fingers.

"It's not much work," he says, "but it does take a steady hand."

"And look how pretty it is!" he says proudly.

"Isn't this much better than a pile of money?" he asks. And everyone agrees. The diamond is much prettier than a dirty pile of money.

"But how does this solve the problem of money?" somebody asks.

"Well," says the stonemason with a smile, "it's like this. We can store as much accumulated labor into one of these little metal-wrapped rocks as we want!"

"Remember," says the stonemason, "the value of money is merely a question of agreement."

"We can store one, a hundred, or even a million labor units into individual bills if we want."

"There is no limit!" he says, "except that it is ugly."

"But if we use diamond rings and other shiny things, then we can store even more—and it will always look good!"

"All we have to do is agree on a value. Whatever we agree to, that is the amount of labor the stone will contain...."

As the stonemason finishes talking there is silence. Brows are furrowed and frowns appear on some of the faces. A buzz of discussion arises and after a few minutes, smiles begin to emerge.

Somebody whispers, "It is brilliant."

But, there are questions.

"What will we do with the money that we store?" asks one.

"And how will we agree on a price?" asks another.

The stonemason smiles and raises his hands.

"I have anticipated these questions and considered a solution," he says with satisfaction. "As for what to do with all the cash, we can build a central storehouse or bank and we can store the money there. As for determining the value of our gold and diamonds, we can appoint our most trusted brothers and sisters to a council and they can determine the price. This council, this cartel if you wish, will tell us, 'a carat of weight is equal to thirty thousand labor units', and we will agree. And as long as we agree," he says with a smile, "we're in business."

The group considers this for a moment. They have to admit, it sounds pretty good. In fact, they cannot see any downside. So, they do it. They create a bank; they create a precious stones and metals cartel; finally, the stonemason gets to work creating new, beautiful, and increasingly extravagant ways to store the money that the people at the top accumulate with increasing efficiency. Problem solved and back to business!

And so, "the band" plays on.

The people at the top of the hill continue their drive for accumulation, distortions pile up, and the people at the bottom work harder and harder just to get by. It seems like a perfect arrangement (at least for the people at the top) and it works beautifully until one day, out of the blue, a financial crisis hits the System like a tsunami hitting the shore.

CRISIS

And I have to say, when that financial tsunami hits, it is a doozy! All of a sudden, and for the first time ever, people at the bottom of hill are out of work. And it isn't in the fancy pants leisured way of those at the top of the hill. It is in an out of money, can't buy enough to eat, lose the house sort of way. When gross unemployment happens, it is a total surprise. One day the economy is working; the next day it isn't. One day people are exchanging goods and services; the next day they aren't. I won't lie to you; the crisis is huge and ugly. Children starve; people die.

Sadly, nobody at the bottom of the hill understands why it is happening. They just know they are suffering. The people at the very tippy top of the hill understand though. They can see the problem as clearly as the diamonds on their fingers. Over the short course of their little accumulation experiment, the  people at the top of the hill have accumulated so much money that they have literally siphoned off all the lifeblood (i.e. cash) from the economy. They have accumulated the dollars and now there isn't any left to lubricate economic exchange. The economy is empty of money and the consequences are tragic. If nobody has money to buy the things they need because all the money has been sucked out of the economy by the people at the top of the hill, and if overspecialization (i.e. moving banana production to one country, and apple production to another) has made barter

67

impossible, how are people going to be able to trade their goods and services? The answer is, they cannot. The bottom line is, if you keep extracting money out of an economy you are gradually and inevitably taking away people's ability to exchange their labor. If you do that for long enough, and aggressively enough, and if you do not put back in all the labor (i.e. money) that you've taken out, then mass unemployment, recession, and economic depression sets in. It is logical, inevitable, and because the ability to barter has been taken away from the people, catastrophic. Millions, even billions, could starve[22] and there is simply nothing, short of total debt repudiation and complete revision of the economic system (i.e. an end to the "right" to accumulate, in other words) that anybody can do to stop it.

---

[22] If you have ever looked up world hunger you get the impression, based on some impressive statistics, that world hunger is on the decline. That is not true. According to the World Food Program Hunger FAQ:

> Whereas good progress was made in reducing chronic hunger in the 1980s and the first half of the 1990s, hunger has been slowly but steadily on the rise for the past decade, FAO said. The number of hungry people increased between 1995-97 and 2004-06 in all regions except Latin America and the Caribbean. But even in this region, gains in hunger reduction have been reversed as a result of high food prices and the global economic downturn that started in 2008.

You can visit the FAQ for updated information on world hunger. World Food Programme, "Frequently Asked Questions," World Food Programme, https://www.wfp.org/hunger/faqs.

Don't believe me?

Let us try a little thought experiment. Imagine for a moment a small economy of ten people. Imagine that each of these ten people has one hundred dollars. Imagine they use their hundred dollars to exchange their labor. Now imagine that one day one of them, let's call him Joe, starts to extract money out of the economy a little bit at a time. Once a week he takes one dollar from each person. Maybe he does it by raising his prices over and above the labor value of his goods. Maybe he does it by taxation. Maybe he starts a stock market[23] and uses that. Maybe he just muscles people into it. How the extraction happens does not matter because the result is always the same. In exactly one hundred weeks Joe will have all the money and everyone else will be empty handed. At that point the other nine people will be unable to exchange their labor because nobody will have any money left to use for exchange. Joe will be fine because he has all the money and he can always command other people to do things for him (like grow him food). Everyone else is in trouble because in a modern monetized world where bananas are grown in Ecuador and

---

[23] The stock market is all about the extraction and accumulation of labor. One experienced stock trader calls extracting labor from others the "Holy Grail" of the stock market. As he or she puts it "Most people don't have the psychological make-up to be traders. It has been said that 80% of traders fail and either quit or lose all their money the first year. This makes perfect sense. The stock market was designed so that the majority will fail. That is the only way that the minority can win." See http://www.swing-trade-stocks.com/grail.html for the remarkably forthright admission.

Apples are grown in Canada, if you don't have money to exchange, you're hooped. Without the ability to exchange their labor, these people will suffer and (if the economy is specialized and nobody grows food nearby) die.

So what is there to do?

Well, if you are one of the nine people who are victims of Joe's jiggery-pokery, you are going to do nothing. To be blunt, if you are not Joe then there is nothing, short of coming up with your own money supply,[24] that you can do. Joe has all the money and only Joe can do something to fix it. The pure and undiluted truth is, if Joe wants to avoid all the nasty human suffering that attends unemployment and recession in an economy that he has sucked dry of its very lifeblood, he has to put all the money that he has extracted back into circulation so that people have the money they need to exchange their labor, period. It is the right thing to do and the only thing that will solve the problem. If Joe doesn't put the money he extracted back into the economy

---

[24] Like they recently tried to do with Bitcoin, which is a nascent alternative medium for labor exchange that currently exists outside of the Family's sphere of influence and control! From the Bitcoin website:

> Bitcoin uses peer-to-peer technology to operate with no central authority or banks; managing transactions and the issuing of bitcoins is carried out collectively by the network. **Bitcoin is open-source; its design is public, nobody owns or controls Bitcoin and <u>everyone can take part</u>**

See <u>https://bitcoin.org</u>. In the context of the discussion in this short essay, Bitcoin may be something important to keep your eye on.

where it belongs, you and the other nine people are out of work, unemployed, and totally and irrevocably screwed.

The million-dollar question is, does Joe put the money back into the economy? The clear and inarguable answer is, no he does not. Joe can clearly see what is happening in the economy and he does feel a little bad about it; but the truth is, he loves the way his life is. He is rich and he can have anything he wants. Of course, the other nine people complain that it is not fair that Joe has extracted all the money and dried up the whole economy, but as we have seen, Joe makes up excuses to justify the situation. Perhaps he convinces himself that the arid economic landscape is an inevitable part of some "economic adjustment." Perhaps he writes it all off as a "cost" of doing business. Perhaps he says things like, "I'm special and chosen by God"[25] or "I've worked so much harder than you therefore I deserve all that money." Perhaps he tells the other nine people in his best Trump voice, "You are a loser," "God doesn't love you," or "You get what you deserve." Perhaps he says nothing at all. It really doesn't matter what excuse he uses because the end result is the same. He convinces himself the crisis is natural and inevitable and he takes absolutely no action at all.

And why should he?

---

[25] Interestingly, as Max Weber pointed out in his classic work *The Protestant Ethic and the Spirit of Capitalism,* and as just about any introductory Sociology text will tell you, "I am special and chosen by God" is the exact argument that Protestants use to justify their wealth. See Max Weber, *The Protestant Ethic and the Spirit of Capitalism* (New York: Roxbury Press, 1904 (1995)).

After all, Joe has lots of money, and he and his family can buy whatever they need to survive. Unemployment is no big deal for him. In fact, unemployment actually works in Joe's favor. The longer people are out of work and the hungrier they get, the more desperate they become. At a certain point the people will be so desperate for food that they will do anything they can in order to feed themselves and their families. Of course, Joe sees this and feels bad. To avoid all the bad feelings, he moves far away from all the suffering so he does not have to see it. He builds castles and moats and he isolates himself away from it all. Ensconced in his extravagant castles and private clubs, he doesn't have to be bothered with the pain and suffering of the masses. Unencumbered by guilt and shame at his actions, he just lets it all unfold.

And I have to say, it gets very bad.

People starve; children die.

The people get angry.

They cry out for assistance.

Joe ignores them.

The people get hungry; the people get desperate.

They gather their pitchforks and scythes.

They light their torches; they build a guillotine, they march up to his castle door,[26] they smash it to bits on the ground,

---

[26] For a nice overview of the proximate causes of the French Revolution, which was the first time the people built a guillotine to deal with Joe and his family, see

and they drag him out into the street. Then, with not a single drop of pity, they chop of his head and he dies.

Of course, this freaks the heck out of Joe's family (let us call them The Family from here on out). They watch as the mob turns to them and they shake in their boots in their castle. They too are dragged out into the street and lined up at the platform. They don't want to die like Joe so they cry and they wail, they beg and they plead.

They make promises; they give assurances.

They apologize for starving the masses.

They swear their loyalty to the people.

Wikipedia, "Causes of the French Revolution," https://en.wikipedia.org/wiki/Causes_of_the_French_Revolutio n. In particular note the sections on the significance of debt. Debt is critical to this economic essay and we will examine the significance of debt below.

The main Wikipedia article on the French Revolution is also enlightening. "The French Revolution," https://en.wikipedia.org/wiki/French_Revolution. The following quote on the causes of the revolution is noteworthy:

> Historians have pointed to many events and factors culminating within the _Ancien Régime_ to lead to the Revolution. Rising social inequality, new political ideas emerging from the Enlightenment, economic mismanagement, environmental factors leading to agricultural failure, **unmanageable national debt** and political mismanagement on the part of King Louis XVI have all been cited as laying the groundwork for the [French] revolution.

They cry out to God in the heavens.

They declare that the bad things will change.

And the mob? Well, they calm down. They are good people after all, God's people, and they don't want to hurt anybody. They just do not like to see their children starve. So, when the family issues apologies, swears oaths, and makes promises, the people want to believe they're sincere, and they do. The Family makes promises and the people believe, not because they are stupid and gullible, but because they are good people and they do not want to hurt anybody. They just want to live in peace! Made hopeful by the promises of the Family, they put down their pitchforks, break down the guillotine, and return to their homes and their places of work and wait to see what the family will do.

GIVING IT ALL BACK

And what does the family do?

Well, after they've returned to their castles, hired extra security, and put bars on their windows and doors, they sit down to think of solutions. Unfortunately, the Family no longer has a choice; they no longer have the luxury of doing nothing. They saw what happened to their Father who art now in heaven and they do not want that to happen to them. So, they think, and they think, and they think. They think that one of the things they could do is pour the money back in. They could empty their accounts, sell off their rock sparkles, and transfuse the economy with the money they took. That would be the right thing to do. All their money came from sucking the economy dry and they rightly should put it back in. If they did that, the economy would spring back to life and the people could live happily

74

ever after. But despite their sworn promise to fix things, they do not do that. Safe in their castles, behind their barred doors, and with the mollified mob put to bed, they realize they do not want to. They like their castles and their parties and their "lifestyle" and they really do not care if the good people starve. They just want what they've "rightfully" earned. Still, they just can't do nothing. If they do nothing, it is only a matter of time before the good people come knocking again, and for obvious reasons the Family does not want that. So, they think and they think and they look for other solutions and one of the first solutions they come up with is force.

FORCE

And that's an obvious one. Clearly the family needs protection. After all, they can't allow themselves to be exposed to what they now tell themselves is a criminal, terrorist, mob. So, they build a police force,[27] they construct

---

[27] There can be no doubt that the police were originally created as a tool to protect the Family by helping them deal with the unrest caused by unfettered accumulation. As noted in Wikipedia, "The first centrally organised police force was created by the government of King Louis XIV in 1667 to police the city of Paris, then the largest city in Europe. The royal edict, registered by the *Parlement of Paris* on March 15, 1667 created the office of *lieutenant général de police* ("lieutenant general of police"), who was to be the head of the new Paris police force, and defined the task of the police as "ensuring the peace and quiet of the public and of private individuals, purging the city of what may cause disturbances, procuring abundance, and having each and everyone live according to their station and their duties."

some jails, they amend their legal code, and they invest in surveillance technology to help keep an eye on the people's unrest. As always, they tax the people to pay for it. Then, in the event of exploding unrest, they arrange for brutality and force (police first,[28] military[29] if needs be). And if the

---

Notice in the bold section how the police are explicitly tasked with ensuring people live according to their "station" (i.e. their social class). This is a fairly unambiguous statement of the repressive and disciplinary purpose of the modern police force.

Note also that the modern uniformed police were first formed in the year 1800 by the emperor Napoléon immediately following the end of the French Revolution! The formation of a professional body of uniformed police controlled by elites in the French state is no mere coincidence. The police were there to help control future revolutionary fervor. See "Police," https://en.wikipedia.org/wiki/Police.

[28] Police, for all the other great things that they do, are always involved in putting down protests in the name of the Family. See for example the police actions and brutality aimed at putting down the Occupy Wall Street movement. Conor Friedersdorf, "14 Specific Allegations of N.Y.P.D. Brutality During Occupy Wall Street," *The Atlantic*2012; Matt Sledge, "Occupy Wall Street Lawsuits Seek Justice for Arrests, Pepper Spray Two Years Later," *Huffington Post* (2013). For a more historical overview, see David Miller and William Dinan, *A Century of Spin*(London: Pluto Press, 2008).

[29] For a particularly unalloyed look at the use of military force to put down protests, see for example John Vidal, "Shell Oil Paid Nigerian Military to Put Down Protests, Court Documents Show " *The Gaurdian*, October 3 2011. You might also want to have a look at how Thailand uses its military to control protest action Nathan Vanderklippe, "Opposition to Thailand's Military Junta Mounts as Even Mildest Protests Shut Down," *The Globe and*

people question the force, which some of them do, thinking it's terribly unfair, the Family can make up excuses, blow up a building or two, or put a dozen police dramas on television to justify their broad use of force.

And it's true isn't it?

Nothing convinces the people of the need for an expanded police and military presence better than a terrorist bomb, a collapsing World Trade center, some media spin,[30] and a Hollywood crime scene or two.

But honestly, even the Family can see that violence and force are not the best way to approach the problem, especially in the Western world where an "at work" labor force and economic stability are what keeps the accumulation regime functioning. Violence might work in a place like Thailand, Syria, or Iraq, but in more "developed" locations, force just leads to instability, and that leads to declining profitability. Remember this: it is always in the best interest of the Family to keep the majority of the people at work. Remember, the Family accumulates labor! Thus the Family only accumulates when people are actually working. If people aren't working, either because they are starving, or in jail, or just fed up, there is no profit; there is no accumulation. In order to ensure the people are willing to work and accumulation moves apace, violence

---

Mail 2015. But don't stop there! If you are interested, use Google to dig up the dirt for yourself.

[30] For a great overview of how the police and media are used in the Family's interest, see Miller and Dinan, *A Century of Spin*.

and force, while ever present as a realizable threat, is always the Family's last resort.

FOOD BANKS

As it turns out, using violence and force as a last resort works well, because there are a lot of other things that the Family can do to prolong their regime. One of the first things they can do is put in place some social welfare. Social welfare, like food banks and green stamps, helps keep protest at bay by controlling the depth of the people's misery. Starving people have nothing to lose and often get agitated and violent as a consequence of their starvation; but a little food, just enough to take the edge off, can keep the people's revolution at bay.[31] And the great thing is, the Family themselves do not have to pay for it! The people at the bottom of the hill are good people after all, and they do not want to see their friends and their families go hungry. So, they open their cupboards and shop a bit harder and when they get to the end of the checkout counter, they drop their donations in the foodbank boxes. And this is great, for the Family, because in this way things do not get so bad. The people do not strictly starve and so they do not pick up pitchforks and knives. But they do suffer. Their caloric intake drops down, their children's physical, emotional, and psychological development stalls,[32] their quality of life

---

[31] Wikipedia has a nice overview of foodbanks and when they emerged. Particularly interesting is the jump in foodbank use since the 2007 financial crisis. Wikipedia, "Foodbank," Wikipedia, https://en.wikipedia.org/wiki/Food_bank.

[32] Poverty and poor nutrition have a "well established" deleterious effect on the emotional, psychological, intellectual, social, and

takes a dive, and they weaken, sicken, and (sometimes) die as a result of the hit.[33] And that's a problem for the Family because even though food banks and food stamps ease the economic hit caused by unfettered accumulation, and prolong their **Regime of Accumulation**[34] as it is, things get worse over time.

Food banks will proliferate, friends and family will suffer, children will grow up small and sick, and eventually the people will put two and two together. They will see the suffering, connect it to accumulation, and get angry and agitated as a result. And of course, that cannot be allowed to happen because as the Family knows, agitation leads to pitchforks and guillotines. So, the Family sits down and

---

even brain(!) development of children. See both H. Yoshikawa, J. L. Aber, and W. R. Beardslee, "The Effects of Poverty on the Mental, Emotional, and Behavioral Health of Children and Youth: Implications for Prevention," *Am Psychol* 67, no. 4 (2012); J. Luby et al., "The Effects of Poverty on Childhood Brain Development: The Mediating Effect of Caregiving and Stressful Life Events," *JAMA Pediatrics* 167, no. 12 (2013).

[33] There is a nice little overview of the impact of diet, nutrition, and poverty on your overall health and wellbeing at Canadian Medical Association, "Health Equity and the Social Determinants of Health," Canadian Medical Association, https://www.cma.ca/En/Pages/health-equity.aspx. **You can also read their report** "What Makes Us Sick," (Canadian Medical Association, 2013). It makes a pretty clear statement about the negative impact of poverty and food insecurity on health and wellbeing.

[34] http://spiritwiki.lightningpath.org/Regime_of_Accumulation.

they think, and they think, and they think, and they come up with more ways to prolong and maintain accumulation.

MANAGING PERCEPTIONS AND EXPECTATIONS

Beyond force and foodbanks, the next thing the Family comes up with is **distraction**.[35] The people can see that pain and suffering are growing around them, but in a modern media saturated world with high Hollywood production value, distracting them and making them think about other things is easy. The beauty industry can distract women by focusing them on their appearance and encouraging them to endlessly tread mill trying to keep up to the airbrushed duplicity of the fashion industry. Men and women can be distracted with sex, gossip, or mindless little internet memes. Hollywood can distract with blockbusters like *The Matrix* or *Hunger Games*, which draw our discontent to the screen and dissipate it in orgiastic emotional rituals of manipulated hope and false pretense. The fitness industry can distract into endless hours of wasted physical exertion.[36] And the distraction goes on and on. The diet industry can distract; sitcoms can distract; police dramas can distract. Even governments can get in on it by distracting people with terrorist threats from half a world away. We truly live in a world of global distraction, and the distraction is good for the Family because it keeps people from thinking about the true realities of accumulation. And that's wonderful

---

[35] See http://spiritwiki.lightningpath.org/Distraction.

[36] Not that exercise is unimportant, but unless you're a competitive athlete, too much exercise is just too much exercise. Past a certain point, exercise doesn't contribute to your overall health and wellbeing.

because as long as the people are not thinking about reality, they are not focused on the costs of accumulation. As long as they are not focused on the cost of accumulation, protest and agitation are kept longer at bay.

Distraction is not the only thing the Family can do to keep the people occupied and inattentive. The Family can also sanitize perception. **Perception Sanitation**[37] is an alteration of individual or collective perception designed to obscure ugly realities. Perception sanitation occurs, basically, when you construct a pretty picture of reality even when reality is an ugly place. For example, when municipal governments clear the homeless from the street so the good people do not have to see the suffering or think about its causes, this is perception sanitation.[38] Similarly, when Hollywood presents images of idyllic family life in rich Bel Air suburbs, when they pimp charming co-ed Friends even while the wealth gap grows and grows,[39] they are engaged (whether their actors are aware of it or not) in perception sanitation. Clearing the streets of the victims of accumulation or presenting images of idyllic family life while sidestepping

---

[37] http://spiritwiki.lightningpath.org/Perception_Sanitation.

[38] See for example Lee Stringer, "We're Hiding the Homeless to Preserve the American Myth," *The Daily Beast* 2014. Sadly, more and more cities are enacting legislation designed to hide the suffering from plain sight.

[39] The *Wealth Inequality* page provides a rather stunning glimpse into the stark reality of wealth inequality. See http://inequality.org/wealth-inequality/. "Wealth Inequality," Inequality.org.

analysis of social issues, sanitizes our perception of reality and confuses us about the extent of the problem.

And it works beautifully!

According to a recent report published by the *National Bureau of Economic Research*, most people have no reasonable picture about the actual economic realities they face. The writers of the report are very clear about their conclusions; most people are clueless.

> In recent years, ordinary people have had little idea about such things. What they think they know is often wrong. Widespread ignorance and misperceptions of inequality emerge robustly, regardless of the data source, operationalization, and method of measurement.[40]

So if most people are clueless about the economic realities they face, what do they think about the economy, reality, and their position in the accumulation regime? The truth is, we are all programmed, as part of the globalized routines of perception sanitation, to believe we are "in the middle," because being in the middle is safe. For example, almost all Hollywood sitcoms are set in middle or upper middle class settings. The only times the lower classes are represented is when they are belittled, as they were in shows like *Married with Children* or even *Malcolm in the Middle.* Belittling the lower/working classes and making them look stupid on television ensures viewers will not

---

[40] Vladimir Gimpelson and Daniel Treisman, "Misperceiving Inequality," *National Bureau of Economic Research Working Paper Series* No. 21174(2015). A quick summary is provide Emily Badger, "People Have No Idea What Inequality Actually Looks Like," *Washington Post* 2015.

want to identify with them. Who wants to identify with the sexist working class fool Ted Bundy, after all?[41] The answer is, nobody. People who see the Hollywood representation identify themselves with the funny, witty, and clean middle class images and not the working class dross.

When you put yourself in the middle, as you are programmed to do by Hollywood media, you do the Family a favor. Being in the middle, you are not so low on the totem pole as to worry or get upset about the situation you are in, and not so high as to be uneasy about the part you are playing. Perceiving yourself as being in the middle makes you calm, grateful (for your position), non-agitated, and generally unlikely to revolt and complain. The problem is of course that more and more people are not in the middle class. The reality is, the middle class has been shrinking for many years now while the rich, and in particular the über rich, increasingly steal the show.[42] Still, as the Hollywood magicians know, it is not reality that matters so much as perception. As long as you believe yourself to be in the middle you are more likely to remain silent, satisfied, and docile.

---

[41] For more on the show *Married with Children,* visit https://en.wikipedia.org/wiki/Married..._with_Children.

[42] See Paul Buchheit, "Infuriating Facts About Our Disappearing Middle-Class Wealth," Moyers and Company, http://billmoyers.com/2014/11/04/infuriating-facts-disappearing-middle-class-wealth/.

INDOCTRINATION

Distraction and perception sanitation keeps us peering at a fantasy image of the world even while the real world collapses around us; but distraction and perception sanitation are not the only things the Family can do. A final thing that the Family can do, other than give the money back, is engage in **indoctrination**.[43] Indoctrination is complex, but it basically involves teaching you to think about the world in a way that encourages you to see the System and what it does as a good thing. When you are indoctrinated, even the worst atrocities perpetrated on humanity by the Family become acceptable. For example, history books (which are commissioned by governments) for a long time taught school children that Native Americans were violent, heathen savages. By teaching that natives were savages, governments[44] were able to justify colonial violence by making it look like they were doing natives a favor by "civilizing them" and bringing them to God. In the case of native North and South Americans, indoctrination involved a dehumanization of the natives and a manipulation of perception in order to cast white colonial violence as beneficent civilization activity. As you may or may not know, it is easy to treat other living beings badly when they do not appear human, and it easy to excuse oppressive acts when we see them as benevolent assistance.

It is notable that this problem of indoctrination still persists today. While few (if any) would depict native North

---

[43] http://spiritwiki.lightningpath.org/Indoctrination.

[44] And always remember, governments control K-12 curriculum.

Americans as savages today, ideological myths that justify colonial violence are still perpetuated. In particular, the myth that all native tribes were nomadic is still prominent in the American K-12 curriculum. However, it is not true. In fact, many native tribes were settled farmers when the Europeans came to take their land. The problem for the Family is, the reality of settled agriculture is hard to reconcile with the colonial pillage of Native lands. The reality is, European colonists came to North America, bumped Native populations off their land, and built their own towns and farms over land they had stolen. By teaching that natives were nomadic, governments et. al, justified colonial pillage by making it look like the natives didn't really own or properly utilize their land to begin with! By telling themselves and their children that natives were all nomadic, the white colonizers created a situation where it became an economic, social, and even moral crime *not* to throw natives on reserves, force march them from their homes,[45] and enclose (read: steal) their lands for white-man use.[46] Viewing colonial violence as a positive, even moral,

---

[45] The *Trail of Tears* is the most infamous forced march of native populations. This occurred in 1838 when the U.S. government, in a move to satisfy the "gold fever" and thirst for expansion of the white colonists, forcibly removed native populations from their farms and homes and force marched them into "Indian territory." Thousands of people died in that forced march. You can search the Internet for "Trail of Tears" to find more information on the tens of thousands of Cherokee, Chickasaw, Choctaw, Creek, and Seminole Indians who lost their homes.

[46] For an overview see John S. Wills, "Popular Culture, Curriculum, and Historical Representation: The Situation of Native Americans in American History and the Perpetuation of

thing is the outcome of indoctrination. As you can see, indoctrination teaches you to see the world in a way that is favorable to the activities of the Family.

Government school curriculum is not the only source of excusatory ideology and indoctrination. The Church, other branches of the State, and Hollywood have been heavily involved in ideological misrepresentation of native populations[47] (and others) in subtle (and not-so-subtle) service to the colonial arm of the System. Even "well meaning" portrayals often end up building up ideology and repressing target populations, most horribly through the actions of our children! A song in the Disney Pocahontas movie called "Savages, Savages" is illustrative:

> What can you expect from filthy little heathens?
> Their whole disgusting race is like a curse.
> Their skin's a hellish red, they're only good when
> dead. They're vermin, as I said.
> And worse.
> They're savages! Savages!
> Barely even human. Savages! Savages!
> Drive them from our shore!
> They're not like you and me

Stereotypes," *Journal of Narrative and Life History* 4, no. 4 (1994).

[47] For an excellent overview, see Anonymous, "Common Portrayals of Aboriginal People," Media Smarts, http://mediasmarts.ca/diversity-media/aboriginal-people/common-portrayals-aboriginal-people. For a look at how damaging the stereotypes are, see Cornel Pewewardy, "The Pocahontas Paradox: A Cautionary Tale for Educators," *Journal of Navajo Education* 14, no. 1-2 (1996).

Which means they must be evil.
We must sound the drums of war!

The lyrics are meant to be an expose of the violent and abusive mentality of the white colonizers, and surely the song-writers never meant it to represent current thinking. In fact, the producers and writers of this movie may have thought they were doing a good thing by exposing the brutal thinking of colonial whites. However, the outcome was opposite and the lyrics actually fanned racist attacks. White children absorbed the song's lyrics and tossed them cruelly back at native children. According to Pewewardy, "Indian children come home in tears - as they have for centuries - when school children or playmates sing "Savages, Savages" to them."[48]

It should be noted here that all the ideological and stereotypical representations of colonized populations are false. Native American's had a sophisticated culture and were very spiritual in their own way. Nevertheless, when European colonists came and took their land, pimped out their children,[49] and in some cases murdered them dead,

---

[48] "The Pocahontas Paradox: A Cautionary Tale for Educators." You can read the article at this address: http://www.hanksville.org/storytellers/pewe/writing/Pocahontas.html.

[49] In a letter written while prisoner on a ship heading to Spain, Christopher Columbus reveals the European pedophilic practices. As he writes, "A hundred castellanos are as easily obtained for a woman as for a farm, and there are plenty of dealers who go about looking for girls; **those from nine to ten are now in demand**, and for all ages a good price must be paid." "Christopher Columbus: The Third Voyage," The Mariners' Museum,

ideology helped justify the blows.[50] Rape, murder, and theft is made acceptable by portraying the natives as, heathen, savage, nomadic, primitives. This is indoctrination. Indoctrination makes us think about the world and the events in it in a way favorable to the Family.

Making you think about the world in a way favorable to the Family (i.e. indoctrinating you) works in a lot of areas of life. When it comes to the economy, accumulation, and in particular debt (see next section), indoctrination ensures that you see the negative consequences of accumulation and debt in a manner favorable to the Family. For example, you may be aware that the economy regularly goes into cardiac arrest and people regularly lose their jobs, their houses, and even their lives. However, you probably do not see this for what it is (i.e. economic malfunction caused by accumulation and debt). Chances are you have been indoctrinated and either

a) ignore it because you've been taught the economy is much too complicated to understand;

b) justify it within an economic framework that normalizes the cardiac dysfunctions as just "business as usual;" or

---

http://ageofex.marinersmuseum.org/index.php?type=explorerse ction&id=65.

[50] You don't have to look very hard on the Internet to find early accounts of atrocities committed against native populations by greedy Europeans. Check out Schilling Vincent, "8 Myths and Atrocities About Christopher Columbus and Columbus Day," *Indian Country*, October 14 2013. Also see James W Loewen, *Lies My Teacher Told Me: Everything Your American History Textbook Got Wrong* (Touchstone, 2009).

c) blame the victim for their failure to successfully compete in the global marketplace.

As a victim of indoctrination you may see the cardiac arrest of your economy not as a sign of increasing economic disease, but as a "correction," a "cyclical downturn," or even as the fault of the people who suffer. While indoctrinated you may conclude that people are homeless and destitute not because the Family has sucked the life-blood out of the economy, but because they were "losers," they "didn't have what it takes," or they were "too weak to compete." It is sad, you will say to yourself, but that's just the way it is. Life is a struggle, people suffer, and that's OK. As the indoctrinated will tell you, suffering builds character, makes you stronger, and teaches you valuable spiritual lessons. So, let it all unfold and do not worry too much about it. Evolution is leading us higher, God is at the helm, and all things happen for a reason.

Do these excuses sound familiar to you?

You may not like to admit it, but if you say these things to explain the economic state of the world, you are indoctrinated. You are viewing the System, accumulation, and the negative consequences of said accumulation in a way that is favorable to the Family. You justify it, excuse it, blame the victim, and otherwise see it as a natural and good thing when it fact (as we shall see below) it is intentional and constructed. When indoctrinated you will see economic downturns, bankruptcies, bailouts, homelessness, misery, austerity measures, and other signs of economic dysfunction in a positive light and you will neither worry about them too much, nor think about them too directly.

I'll speak more about indoctrination and its consequences when I speak about old and new energy archetypes below. For now, I'll simply conclude by saying that indoctrination is a powerful mechanism of prolonging accumulation that works by negating the people's suffering and turning it into a good thing. When combined with distraction and perception sanitation, indoctrination can go a long way towards keeping your attention turned away from the key issues. Of course, the Family is not going to call all this distraction, sanitation, and indoctrination. That would just leave the people bitter and alarmed. Instead, the Family will use words like "entertainment," "education," and "fashion," or they will wrap their ideology and sanitation in religious, scientific, and Hollywood clothing. They may even get together and give themselves awards for all the good work they are doing. But no matter how many awards they give themselves, and no matter what they name their activities, the end result is the same. The people are diverted and the Family's regime continues on and on.

DEBT

Using force, indoctrination, perception sanitation, and so on do prolong accumulation. Unfortunately for the Family, these are all just bandage solutions. They do not solve the main problem, which is that the Family is accumulating money out of the economy, and so they always fail because sooner or later the Family has extracted all the money, and the economic bloodstream dries up. At that point unemployment, recession, and suffering intensify, the people get agitated, and discontent and violence may erupt. And even if the revolution is eventually put down, it is never good for the Family. Revolution halts accumulation (because the people are not working), targets Family members, and wastes a lot of money. The Family knows this and they know they have to do more than just use ideology and indoctrination to confuse, mollify, and misdirect. The question is, what can they do?

As it turns out, and as much as they do not want to, the Family must put money back into the economy in one way or another. They have no other choice. If they do not put at least some money back into the economy, the economy eventually dries up, and suffering, unemployment, and agitation grows. It is inevitable and so at some point, they must add money back in. The only question is, how do they do it?

Well, the Family does not want to just "give it away." That is, they don't want to just dump the money they took back in. They "earned" their cash, they tell themselves, and it just wouldn't be fair to ask them to sacrifice all their hard work for the "lazy people" who suffer now.[51] More of a problem, if they just gave it back, it might set a precedent, and the people might come to expect it. Then, every time accumulation shuts down the economy, the people would expect the Family to give back. And giving it back is never appealing to the Family. So, after some lavish private parties and some recondite economical thought, they came up with a perfect economic solution. In order to jump start the dying economy, the Family would simply lend their money back in!

And what a beautiful solution that was! The Family has been accumulating for centuries and they have wads of cash just sitting around with nothing to do. Therefore, thought the Family, they could lend it to the people. If they did that, the people would have money to exchange and the economy would be working again. Problem solved, life goes on, except for one problem. Although the Family knew they had to lend money to get the economy working, they didn't want to just give it up and ask for it back at a later date. Their basic concern was, what was in it for them?

---

[51] Like the government blamed the natives for being savages, the rich often blame the poor for being too lazy and uneducated to support themselves and work. In this way they absolve themselves of responsibility for economic crisis and blame the victims for a fate foisted upon them by the Family's accumulation regime. But, it is not true. People are out of work and suffering not because they are lazy, but because the System of accumulation has sucked the economy dry and left them neither the power to trade, or the hope to even try. For a rundown of the proximate causes of poverty, see this wonderful blog post by *The Borgen Project*.
http://borgenproject.org/what-causes-global-poverty/.

It was "their" money after all and lending it out meant they couldn't enjoy it for themselves. They liked showing off their bank accounts and their bling and so they would be making a huge sacrifice in the process. And besides, God would not be happy if they just gave it all back. Handouts do not make you strong, they told themselves, and there is no life lesson in charity. And so, not wanting to just hand it out, they think and they think and they eventually come up with a brilliant idea called **interest.**[52] In order to keep the monetary bloodstream flowing, the Family would lend out their money at interest. They would lend a hundred bucks and they would get back one hundred and ten. And that would solve all their issues. They would get something in return for their sacrifice, the people would learn a valuable life lesson, and the economy would chug back to life.

It was a beautiful and darkly brilliant idea.

So...

The Family called the people to assembly and they announced their perfect solution. In order to get the economy working again, they would lend money to the people and the people would pay them back with interest.

"We'll lend you a hundred, you'll get back to work, and you'll give us a hundred and ten!" said an excitedly bright and sanguine speaker.

The people listened, and at first they were confused. Indeed, at first it seemed like a perfectly absurd idea. They could understand why the Family would want the original one hundred back, "But why interest?" asked the people.

---

[52] http://spiritwiki.lightningpath.org/Interest.

"Well," says the speaker, "we figure that since we are letting you use 'our' money, we are making a huge sacrifice."

"You see", he says with gravity, "we worked hard for the cash and we earned it quite fair. If we give it to you what's in it for us while we share?"

And at his words the people pause and they think and their puzzled looks drain quickly away. They understand, it is a sacrifice for the Family to lend out their money, and it seems only fair that they get something in return. And really, even if they don't like it, the people have no other choice. They either take the money and agree to the interest, or the economy stays drained and they starve; so they smile, they shake hands, they agree to pay interest, and they take for themselves some of the "Family's" own money.

And thankfully, lending money does the trick. With money transfused back in, everyone gets straight back to work and everybody is happy once again. Unfortunately, the party doesn't last very long. In fact, this time it shuts down much, much sooner. The problem is, the Family has fangs in the economic jugular in two ways now. On the one hand they are still engaged in their regular extractive activities and these activities once again drain the economy; on the other hand they are getting interest payments on the loans used to keep the economy moving, and this drains the economy as well! Extraction and accumulation now happens on two fronts, with predictable and inevitable, results. The Family gets even richer even faster, and the economy smashes to a halt even sooner—except this time it is worse. Because the people are using borrowed money, and because that money comes with an interest charge, when all the money has been sucked out the people are left with less than nothing at all! Indeed, when all the money is extracted, the people are left with **debt**.

THE PROBLEM WITH DEBT

Debt, debt, debt.

And what's the problem with debt?

Debt is the bane of our existence.

Debt is the source of our despair.

Debt is bad, and that's the bottom line. When debt is introduced into the accumulation equation, people regularly end up with less than nothing at all, even though they work their entire lives to build something up. It is horrible, perverse, absurd, and ridiculous; it is all the more so because the problem with debt goes beyond the crushing "nothing" that accompanies the people into their graves. You see, debt is also a problem for the Family as well because debt deepens (some economists would say causes) the crisis.[53] The problem is, when people are mired

_____

[53] That debt is the main economic problem of our times, and the engine of our despair and destruction, is made crystal clear in a recent paper by Alan Taylor for the National Bureau of Economic Research. In this paper, Taylor argues that **private debt** is the principle cause of all major financial crises Eli M Noam, *Media Ownership and Concentration in America*(New York: Oxford University Press, 2009). If you want an easy to read run down of the main points of the article, and the serious implications, see
Camilla Cornell, "The Real Cost of Raising Kids," *Money Sense*, June 11 2011.

in debt, the Family loses **confidence** in the people's ability to pay back any money they may receive. Family members are not stupid after all. They know that if they lend money to people in debt, people may default and they may never get their "investment" back. Debt thus makes the Family unwilling to lend into the economy—it is just too risky. With debt in the picture, when the economy dries up, the Family refuses to lend and things get much, much worse than before. Remember, the only way to jump-start an economy starved of money is to put money back in. Also remember, the only way the Family is willing to do that is to lend at interest. If the people are in too much debt and the Family is not willing to lend, then nothing short of giving the money back, can jump start the dying economy.

And I have to say, when debt enters the picture and takes away the Family's confidence, the crisis can get very bad indeed. People starve, children die, and a mob begins to develop. Of course, the Family may be tempted to ignore them, but they know they cannot get away with that forever. Eventually, the mob gets pitchforks and scythes. It has happened before and the Family knows that if things get bad enough, it will happen again. If you doubt this, just look at the most recent example from Syria where anger at the "failure of long-promised economic and political reforms"[54] has led to revolutionary violence and "systematic collapse and destruction." The economic foundations of Syria have been destroyed and "its infrastructure and institutions, human and physical capital,

---

[54] "10 Simple Points to Help You Understand the Syria Conflict," *News.com.au* 2013.

as well as the wealth of the nation has been obliterated."[55] It is not a pretty global picture, especially when we consider Syria is not the only nation on the brink of systemic collapse. Heather Steward, for example, provides a list of over 30 countries in economic jeopardy at the present time. And note, Steward suggests that the problem is not just in the developing world. Her organization found that "net cross-border lending worldwide, including the private sector as well as governments, has increased from $11.3 trillion in 2011 to $13.8tn in 2014 – and forecasts that it will reach $14.7tn this year."[56] There is no other way to say it but that a staggering amount of debt exists in the world today.

RESTORING CONFIDENCE

With economy mired in debt and on the brink of collapse, what does the Family do? As always, they gather in private[57] and they think and they think and they think. They think for a good long time until finally it hits them. The problem isn't that they are siphoning money, and the problem isn't that the people are being driven into the grinding

---

[55] Syrian Center for Policy Research, "Alienation and Violence: Impact of Syria Crisis Report 2014,"(United Nations, 2014), 6.

[56] See Heather Stewart, "Beyond Greece, the World Is Filled with Debt Crises," July 11 2015.

[57] One of the more infamous private gatherings of Family members is the *Bilderberg Group*. There is a total media blackout around this yearly meeting of the über rich and powerful, and nobody knows what they talk about but them. For a quick overview, see. "Bilderberg Group," Wikipedia, https://en.wikipedia.org/wiki/Bilderberg_Group.

desolation of debt, the problem is the Family has no confidence! The problem is, the people are so riddled with debt that the Family knows they will never be able to pay it back. As a result, the Family has no confidence in the people's ability to pay. Without confidence in the people's ability to pay, nobody wants to lend any money. If the Family could just restore confidence, then they'd all be willing to lend and the problem would finally be solved! The only question is, how do they restore their own confidence?

Well, after some gourmet eats and high-end treats they come up with a few things to do. One of the **first things** that the Family does is "reset" the economy. They do this by simply letting the economy collapse and then clawing everything back in a process they call **deleveraging**.[58] Deleveraging is really just the process of selling assets to cover debt. In other words, when the economy crashes, people sell things to get cash, and the Family buys it back, usually at pennies on the dollar. The more the Family is able to cash in on the bargains, the more their confidence in an economic reset builds. And I have to say, the deals are great. The debt riddled people sell their houses, their cars, their businesses, and anything else they can get their hands on in order to service their debt and survive the crisis. And if they are not willing to sell, there is always the law. If the people are reluctant to give things up, legal means can be used to repossess their goods.

Of course, and as you might expect, deleveraging can be a very cruel process for those who lose everything, but the Family carries on. The Family reasons that the people

_____

[58] http://spiritwiki.lightningpath.org/Deleveraging.

borrowed money to buy houses, cars, and businesses and since they cannot pay the Family back, it is only fair that they take what is theirs. And boy, do they take. They take back businesses; they take back houses; they take back cars; indeed, they take back everything that they can. No matter what the cost to the people, the Family takes. They do this not because they are mean and greedy (or so they tell themselves), but because they are just trying to restore the necessary confidence.

Taking things back, i.e. deleveraging, works for a while; but unfortunately, that's not enough. During the first few major crises it was. During the first few crises, forcing the people to deleverage was sufficient to restore confidence. But the problem is the debt crisis is cyclical and it gets worse every time. Every time the Family lends money at interest, every time the economy crashes, the debt hole gets deeper and wider. Eventually debt is so bad that even governments (who regularly borrow money to try and cope with the Family's incessant accumulation) can't afford to pay. When the Family loses confidence in the government, that's a very, very bad day because the Family just can't cut governments off completely like they might do to the people. Cutting governments off from the money supply that the Family controls through their system of centralized *banks* would mean that governments would not have the funds to function. If governments didn't have the funds to function, they wouldn't be able to perform important services, like controlling the military, managing the police, ensuring roads are maintained so goods can flow, disciplining commercial transactions, funding prisons, and so on. If governments cannot perform important functions, the political, economic, and social order would collapse very quickly. If the political, economic, and social order collapses, masses of people would be thrown out of work, mass suffering would occur, and revolution would quickly ensue as it did in Syria, and as it has done elsewhere. And that's bad, especially if the government isn't around to control things. If the government isn't around to control the military and handle the police, pitchforks, pokey sticks, and guillotines emerge. Therefore, and at all reasonable costs, the Family must maintain confidence in the government.

Of course, maintaining confidence in the government means having faith in the government's ability to pay for their debt, and that can be a problem especially when debt is so high that even large and developed countries can no longer pay. But the Family has a plan. When debt is so bad that even governments can't pay, the Family can impose **austerity**.[59] The family tells governments that they won't lend them any more money unless they cut back their spending so that there's more money to service the debt. It is just like in your own household. If you are loaded down with interest payments, you have to cut back on spending in order to make sure you can make your debt payment.

The issue is, the Family doesn't require (or even want) the government to cut back on all types of spending. The Family only wants the government to cut back on

---

[59] As they did most recently in Greece. See for example. Phillip Inman, Graem Wearden, and Helena Smith, "Greece Debt Crisis: Athens Accepts Harsh Austerity as Bailout Deal Nears," *The Gaurdian* July 9(2015). I really recommend you look at this article online. At this point you'll have no trouble understanding clearly what the Greece crisis is about.

education, healthcare, social programs, and other "unnecessary" (for the Family, anyway) luxuries. For reasons that should be obvious at this point, the Family does not want the government to cut back on police and military force and surveillance. The Family needs these just in case things go south. But cutting programs to the people, that is OK; and thankfully, that works! Invoking austerity by cutting things like education, health care, and social programs ensures governments have the revenue flow to service their debt and maintain those services (like the police and the penal system) that help ensure the Family's safety. Austerity helps keep Family confidence high and the money transfusion flowing. True, like deleveraging, austerity measures cause a lot of suffering, and they make things much worse in the long run, but it would be a lot worse if the government lost control. As long as the government is in control, the economy can chug along and force (i.e. police/military) can be used to control the angry mobs that inevitably develop. It is not a perfect solution, and as we will see below it cannot go on like this forever (especially since debt levels are set to reach WWII levels in the next few years), but by forcing deleveraging, imposing austerity, and using force whenever they need to, the Family can squeeze a long time before things get totally out of hand.[60]

---

[60] I should note at this point that deleveraging and austerity do nothing but further wreck an economy already wrecked by perpetual accumulation. Following the 2009 austerity measures, Greek debt climbed from 126 percent of GDP to 177 percent of GDP, putting the Greek economy in even worse shape. The Family may have got their money back, but the country had to pay the price. As Paul Krugman notes, the rise in debt was not

Deleveraging and austerity are two things the Family can do to maintain their confidence in the economy. The third thing that the Family can do to maintain confidence is print money. That is, instead of lending their own money the Family can simply take control of the process and print it out as they need to. Printing more money is a great way to stave off economic collapse because it ensures a continual supply of cash into an economy continually drained by accumulation. All the Family has to do is setup a central national bank, give that bank a license to print money, and then let it go. Once the bank is setup, other smaller banks (also controlled by members of the Family) can borrow money from the central bank and lend that out to the people, at interest of course. The Family benefits in two ways. On the one hand they benefit because they don't use their own money and so they are in no risk of losing it. The Family benefits in another way as well because even though they print money out of thin air, they still charge interest on that money, and that's great because that is literal financial black magic. When the Family starts to accumulate money they create out of thin air they begin to accumulate in a third way. Remember, the Family accumulates raw labor in the form of profit, they accumulate interest on money they lend, and now they accumulate interest magically based on the money they print out and lend. What a deal, what a deal, what a deal!

---

the result of out of control borrowing, it was the result of declining GDP caused by measures beneficial to the Family, but damaging to the Greek economy as a whole. Paul Krugman, "Debt Deflation in Greece," *New York Times*, July 7 2015.

Of course, the Family might say that the people benefit as well. Connecting the economic body up to a permanent, interest-bearing cash intravenous (IV) does stave off the inevitable economic collapse caused by the extractive activities of the Family and it does keep the economy chugging along; but it is not a permanent solution because, like lending their own money at interest, it actually deepens the crisis. This is because lending money at interest *always* causes more debt, and debt is what is shutting the economy down. The problem is exacerbated when the Family starts printing money because now that they don't have to use their own money, their confidence levels can be quite low and they will still lend out money! In fact, when they start printing money confidence can approach zero and they will still lend because even the act of printing money generates accumulation for them. If they print 100 dollars and they get even 10 dollars back, it is still profit for them! Of course, lending their own money and printing it magically out of thin air means more debt; and, more debt means a deeper crisis. Eventually the debt hole will be so big and confidence will be so low that the economy will simply shut down, and that will be the end of it. And notably, the problem is not just a spiraling chasm of debt. Inflation, which is a factor that enters the equation as the direct result of the printing of money to cover debt, also exacerbates the problem. Inflation amplifies the crisis by devaluing the Family's money![61] Couple inflation with the growing

---

[61] How does printing money cause inflation and devalue the Family's money? Imagine our little economy of ten people, each with a hundred dollars. After all the money has been extracted, the people can't work. Joe, being the good guy that he is, lends them some of "his" money at twenty percent interest. Work goes

problem of debt and you have a perverse economic system that cycles in and out of deepening economic crisis with increasing rapidity and severity.

If this all sounds absurd, it is. But under economic regimes that encourage accumulation, it is a fact of life. As Alan Taylor notes "the historical record appears to present us with a rather inconvenient truth, namely that financial crisis might just be an occupational hazard, a simple fact of life

---

on, Joe extracts, and the economy is drained again. However, since money was lent at interest, the second time around Joe has to lend $120.00 to each. When the economy fails again his buddies owe him $150.00. Pretty soon he has to lend $200.00, $400.00, and even more, just to kick-start the economy. The problem is, this devalues Joe's money. It has to do with the ratio of money in the economy to the available labor. Let us simplify. Let us imagine that in Joe's economy people work a total of one hundred hours a year. Let us say that economy needs a total of 1,000 x 10 or $10,000 dollars in the economy to be fully monetized (ten people working a total of 1,000 hours a year is 10,000 labor units and hence $10,000). With $10,000 dollars in the economy it costs one dollar to buy one hour of labor. If, at the point of reset, Joe has ten thousand dollars in the bank, that gives him the ability to control ten thousand hours of labor. But now imagine that after a few rounds of crises and reset, Joe has to print $40,000 dollars into the economy just to cover available labor. With $40,000 representing the 10,000 hours of labor, it will now cost four dollars to buy one hour of labor. At that point Joe is going to be able to command only twenty-five hundred hours of labor with his $10,000 dollars, a significant reduction. This is a devaluation of Joe's money. This is inflation.

in modern finance capitalism."[62] Just how much of a hazard this is for the people can be seen by the last big financial meltdown in 2007. In the years that followed that crisis, the Family imposed incredible suffering, and deleveraged and extracted trillions of dollars, in an effort to restore confidence. As Elitsa Vucheva notes: "In April of 2009, it was reported that, 'EU governments have committed 3 trillion Euros [or $4 trillion dollars] to bail out banks with guarantees or cash injections in the wake of the global financial crisis...'"[63] In actuality, four trillion is a drop in the bucket. The real number, according to Andrew Gavin Marshall, is closer to $25 trillion![64] That is a staggering amount of money. The fact that it was funnelled to a few members of the Family while millions suffer is a ridiculous example of greed, graft, and the absurdity of the System. Think about this. That single "transfer" from that single crisis could (should it simply be put back into circulation where it belongs) easily and unambiguously solve not only the global financial crisis, but also all the current problems (like hunger, housing, unemployment, etc.) that we, as a human race, face.[65] It is no understatement to say that our world is a world of Panglossian absurdity.

---

[62] Alan M. Taylor, "The Great Deleveraging," in *The Social Value of the Financial Sector*, ed. Viral V. Acharya(Hackensack, NJ: World Scientific Publishing, 2014), 48-9.

[63] Elitsa Vucheva "European Bank Bailout Total: $4 Trillion," *Bloomberg Business*, April 10 2009.

[64] Andrew Gavin Marshall, "Entering the Greatest Depression in History," *Global Research*, August 6 2009.

[65] Giving all that money back to the people requires a certain faith in humanity. Unfortunately, faith in humanity is one of the things

APOCALYPSE

That cyclic hardship for the people is a "fact of life," and that the Family steals trillions from public coffers, is bad enough; but it is not just cyclic economic hardship that people have to deal with. Because of the accumulating black hole of debt, recessive crises happen with more frequency, and unfold with greater depth, each time they occur. The problem is, any solution provided by the Family doesn't solve the issue (which is accumulation), it

---

that the Family totally lacks. In their rambling efforts to provide excuse and justification for centuries of accumulation, the Family has developed all sorts of BS representations of human nature. They have gotten their priests (or in modern times, members of The Institute) to tell lies about "original sin" and "unevolved apes". They have portrayed humans as sinful, violent, rejects. They have told us we are in a cosmic school, here to learn our karmic lessons. They have created churches and lodges to convince themselves and indoctrinate others, and movies, like *2001 A Space Odyssey, A Clockwork Orange*, or even *The Sphere,* to drive it all home. Indeed, *2001 A Space Odyssey* is a great example of Family ideology designed to paint the masses as violent and primitive apes in need of totalitarian control. Just watch the opening sequence to see the Family's view of you! From the opening sequence to the nuclear destruction at the end the message is clear. It is your violent and ape like nature that is the cause of the global shit storm we are all about to endure, unless something changes very fast.

I feel, at this point, compelled to point out that the Family's view of human nature is not true. Contrary to their BS, humans are in fact wired for altruism and compassion. If you have time I recommend you watch the *Canadian Broadcasting Corporation* (CBC) documentary, *Born to be Good?* It is available at http://www.cbc.ca/natureofthings/episodes/born-to-be-good-1

postpones the inevitable collapse and exacerbates the tsunami when it hits. The reality is, under the Family's regime of accumulation, debt always expands and the crises always deepens. If this goes on long enough pretty soon debt is so outrageously high, and the crisis so intractably deep that it becomes almost impossible to restore confidence. We might call the point where the crises is so deep that it is impossible to restore confidence the **über-crises**.[66] When the über-crises finally hits, the world ends.[67]

And the funny thing is, the Family knows all about this (though they may not want to admit it). As Balzli and Schiessle note of the previous economic meltdown, "the central bankers knew exactly what was going on, a full two-and-a-half years before the big bang."

---

[66] http://spiritwiki.lightningpath.org/Uber-Crises.

[67] The global economic crisis of 2007 came pretty close to being the über-crises. It was so bad that in order to keep things running, the Family has had to lend money at 0 percent interest! Lending money at 0 percent is something that is anathema to the Family, so you know that things were very bad indeed.

As I write this today is December 16, 2015. On this day in history the United States Reserve bank is expected to raise interest rates "exactly seven years after the central bank cut them to almost zero in response to the deepest recession in the post-World War II era." And this only on very weak employment statistics! I guess the Family is getting impatient "giving" money away. With debt reaching WWII levels and the globe teetering on the brink of war, the next couple of years should be very interesting indeed. For an overview see Jeanna Smialek, "Here's What 7 Years at Zero Rates Have Looked Like," *Bloomberg Business* 2015.

> It was probably the biggest failure of the world's central bankers since the founding of the BIS in 1930. They knew everything and did nothing. Their gigantic machinery of analysis kept spitting out new scenarios of doom, but they might as well have been transmitted directly into space.[68]

Because of their privileged financial vantage point, the Family can see it coming better than anybody. The problem is, they are caught in a proverbial Gordian knot. "Traditional wisdom" says it is lax lending practices (i.e. cheap money), loose transfusion practices, and even stupid human nature that is the cause.[69] "Traditional wisdom" says in order to fix the problem you need to control lending, control spending, manage debt, and work to overcome the stupidity of the mob. If you do that, everything will be OK. Unfortunately, most (if not all) of the things the Family says are "traditional wisdom" are neither traditional nor wise. Most often "traditional wisdoms" are merely the excuses they use to cover up their accumulation scam. In reality, nothing they do, short of giving all the money back, can solve the problem. No matter what sort of economic skullduggery they engage in and no matter how creatively they blame the people, as long as they continue to accumulate, debt is going to grow, crisis is going to deepen, and a global crisis of devastating proportions is eventually (some might say already is) going to occur. Truly, the global

---

[68] Beat Balzli and Michaela Schiessl, "The Man Nobody Wanted to Hear: Global Banking Economist Warned of Coming Crisis," *Spiegel International* (2009).

[69] Ibid.

collapse of 2007 is a just a way station on the way to apocalyptic financial meltdown.

And do not kid yourself, the Family can see it coming. IMF databases clearly show rising rates of debt *and clearly demonstrate* that financial crisis coincide with high levels of debt.[70] What is most troubling is that since debt reached its highest levels ever in 2007-8 (the exact point of the last financial crisis) it is rising fast again. Global debt has risen by over $100 trillion since the last crisis, driven in large measure by government and corporate borrowing.[71] Indeed, as I write these words, public and private debt have sent at least twenty-four nations into debt crisis,[72] while another 71 may be rapidly on their way.[73] How many of these will end up like Syria is anybody's guess, but clearly it is bad and getting worse.[74] Peter Spence points out just how serious and intractable the problem is becoming.

---

[70] View an IMF infographic of debt at ww.imf.org/external/pubs/ft/fandd/2011/03/pdf/picture.pdf

[71] John Glover, "Global Debt Exceeds $100 Trillion as Governments Binge, Bis Says," *Bloomberg Business* March 9(2014).

[72] Michael Snyder, "The Bankruptcy of the Planet Accelerates – 24 Nations Are Currently Facing a Debt Crisis," *Global Research* (2015).

[73] Tim Jones, "The New Debt Trap: How the Response to the Last Global Financial Crisis Has Laid the Ground for the Next,"(Jubilee Debt Campaign, 2015).

[74] Michael Snyder, "16 Facts About the Tremendous Financial Devastation That We Are Seeing All over the World," *Global Research* June 29(2015).

> The world will be unable to fight the next global financial crash as central banks have used up their ammunition trying to tackle the last crises, the Bank for International Settlements has warned. The so-called central bank of central banks launched a scatching [sic] critique of global monetary policy in <u>its annual report</u>. The BIS claimed that central banks have backed themselves into a corner after repeatedly cutting interest rates to shore up their economies.[75]

As should be crystal clear at this point, distraction, indoctrination, sanitation, austerity, transfusion, repossession of goods, and all the other tools in the Family's economic arsenal can only work so long. Eventually things are going to get really bad and dominoes are going to fall. If you think that the Syrian refugee crisis, the Middle East, ongoing economic meltdowns, and anguish/suffering is bad now, you just wait. If the Family continues business as usual, it is all going to get worse on an accelerating exponential curve.

So what can you do? What can the Family do? As Spence notes, the Family has exhausted their options.[76] Really the only option now is to <u>wake up</u>, admit to the greedy, corrupt, twisted nature of the System, repudiate all debt, cap accumulation, outlaw interest, and allow the world to live happily ever after. If the Family does this, then we can all sing, "For he's a jolly good fellow" and go dance in the streets. If the Family makes that choice, it will mean a permanent end to poverty and suffering and the global

---

[75] Peter Spence, "The World Is Defenceless against the Next Financial Crisis, Warns Bis," *The Telegraph* (2015).

[76] Ibid.

emergence of Shambhala and utopia. Just imagine what kind of world we could all live in if a) we didn't have to struggle with debt; b) all the money that had been extracted was returned into the economy; and c) we suddenly had all the money we needed to exchange our labor. With modern technological wizardry such as it is, a single hour of labor goes a long, long way! Multiply an hour of technologically enhanced labor power by the 7 billion people of this planet and you have a utopian powder keg. I have no doubt that we could easily build a new world in less than a single generation if the Family simply released their hold. Of course, and despite what those people behind the Zeitgeist might suggest, we need a lot more than just technology to create Utopia. The Family's economy has caused a lot of pain and anger, a lot of hurt and oppression, and a lot of damage and psychosis. For the first little while a lot of the available money would have to go to healing the human body and restoration of the global landscape. But that would be fun, especially if coupled with full awareness of the nature of that work, and full support for the healers that do the work. And it wouldn't have to go on forever. The body, whether it is the body of Gaia, or the body of humans, is remarkably resilient. Change its toxic environment, give it the truth about things, and offer it a helping hand when necessary, and it heals quickly and naturally.

On the other hand, the Family could (and probably will) try to continue in the old ways, try to hang onto their money, and try to retain their regime of accumulation. They will probably suggest minor policy revisions, a bandage here and there, and a tweak or two up and down the economic pipe. They will point to low interest rates, quantitative easing, corporate inversions, or any of a host of other things to divert attention from the real issue, which is accumulation. They will engage in bailouts and handouts and sell outs and they will desperately try to find increasingly absurd ways to defibrillate the global economy whenever it goes into cardiac arrest.[77] Their tweaking may prolong the inevitable a bit longer, but at a certain point a global financial meltdown of biblical proportions will occur and there will be nothing the Family can do to stop it. It will probably start in a single sector of the consumer economy with a "normal" reset and recession. However, because the rest of the economy is mired in debt, the recession will not stay confined to a single sector. Even a little drop off in sales will trigger bankruptcy and default in other sectors. With debt so deep, the dominoes will fall and the global economy will go into cardiac arrest, with predictable and disastrous consequences for the majority of people. The suffering, misery, discord, and violence could be apocalyptic.[78]

---

[77] The most recent absurdity is negative interest rates. I'm not going to deal with this here except to say that if the Family is considering negative interest rates, the global situation must be very bad indeed. For an introduction see Rochelle Younglai, "What Are Negative Interest Rates and How Do They Work? ," *The Globe and Mail*, December 9 2015.

[78] If there is one gene that Family members lack, it is the gene of accountability. They don't like to take responsibility for the things they have done, probably because to do so would put their "balance sheet" in the red for a long, long, long time. Therefore, when the Family begins to realize they have lost all control, they will desperately look around for somebody else to blame. They will try to blame human nature, human failings, "socialist"

I hate to say it here, but from my current vantage point, it looks like the Family knows this is coming. It also looks like rather than do the right thing they are just upping their image management, consolidating their police and military forces, increasing global surveillance,[79] putting repressive

---

spending, primitive leanings, Muslim terrorists, or even God. They will say things like "This is an act of God," "God is punishing us," or "This is part of our 'lesson' plan." They will even, as one government leader recently said in Alberta, Canada, where I am from, blame you directly for the crisis. In a blatant and classic statement of the Family's avoidant personality disorder, premier Jim Prentice, when asked about the causes of the current financial crises, told us all to "look in the mirror". He said, and I quote, "in terms of who is responsible, we need only look in the mirror. **Basically, all of us have had the best of everything and have not had to pay for what it costs.**" Classic Family rhetoric! They blame the economic crisis, a crisis caused by their own accumulation activities, on the people at the bottom of the hill who are themselves the actual victims of accumulation.

On the Family's attempts to avoid accountability I only have to two things to say. **One**, don't buy it. As should be evident at this point, it is the accumulation regime of the Family that is the cause of our financial woes. **Two**, when the Family does finally choose to be accountable and change the System (and they will), let it go. Forgive, forget, and move on to the job of building utopia. Holding grudges, throwing people in jail, and engaging in violent acts of retribution are counterproductive. What we need, as I will argue below, is healing, education, and awareness and not more suffering, violence, and woe.

"#Prenticeblamesalbertans Goes Viral after Jim Prentice's 'Look in the Mirror' Comment," *CBC News Edmonton* 2015.

[79] Global surveillance refers to the "mass surveillance of entire populations across national borders." It is rooted in the

laws in place,[80] and otherwise getting ready for the global chaos that will ensue (that some would say is already ensuing) as the global economy collapses.[81] Judging by the increasingly violent actors on the global "checkerboard," it also looks like they are getting ready for a third (and final, according to eschatological spirituality) world war. Indeed, sadly, and as others have said,[82] global war looks increasingly planned, and increasingly inevitable.

---

development of a global security network. World elites denied the existence of this network for many years, but it was finally disclosed as fact when Edward Snowden went rogue and disclosed the extent of global surveillance. You can read more at Wikipedia, "Global Surveillance,"
https://en.wikipedia.org/wiki/Global_surveillance.

[80] For example, recent legislation in Spain bans public demonstration outright. This legislation, which was "passed in parliament last December despite all groups except for the ruling conservative PP (Partido Popular) voting against the legislation" is, according to many, "the worst news for Spanish Democracy since the dictator Franco." "Spanish Government Cracks Down on Right to Demonstrate – Security or Repression?," *Euronews* 2015.

[81] You can keep up with the Family's repressive practices by following *Human Rights Watch* (https://www.hrw.org/) or *Amnesty International* (https://www.amnesty.org/en/latest/).

[82] Paul Craig Roberts, a former research fellow at Stanford University's *Hoover Institution* and a globally respected political analyst, speaks with some horror about the "drive to war" currently underway.

And just why would I say that a global WWIII is planned? Well, as the Family discovered a long time ago, not only is war a great way to channel the agitated aggression of the suffering people at the bottom of the hill, it is also a great way to pull an economy out of catastrophic depression and debt. War allows the Family to inject big money into the economy in a way that does not give their secret (the real secret) away, i.e. that accumulation is occurring, and that

---

See Paul Craig Robers, "War Is Coming — Paul Craig Roberts," http://www.paulcraigroberts.org/2014/07/28/war-coming-paul-craig-roberts/.

Also, Kyle Bass, founder of Hayman Capital Management, writes about the coming financial and political apocalypse:

> Trillions of dollars of debts will be restructured and millions of financially prudent savers will lose large percentages of their real purchasing power at exactly the wrong time in their lives. Again, the world will not end, but the social fabric of the profligate nations will be stretched and in some cases torn. Sadly, looking back through economic history, all too often war is the manifestation of simple economic entropy played to its logical conclusion. We believe that war is an inevitable consequence of the current global economic situation.

See Kyle Bass, "Hayman Capital Letters,"(Hayman Capital Management, 2012). The 2012 "letter" is available online at https://www.scribd.com/doc/113621307/Kyle-Bass

One author has collected a long and fascinating list of quotations and factoids about the apparent ramp up to WWII. Because of the nature of the above source you are advised to check and double check the factoids and quotes before believing they are real. You can read it at WashingtonsBlog, "Why We're Sliding Towards World War," Information Clearning House, http://www.informationclearinghouse.info/article43538.htm.

accumulation is the reason for the crisis. And we are not talking about a localized little conflict here. At the point of total economic collapse, the Family is going to need a real war, a global war, with gadjillions of dollars in military spending leading to bajillions of dollars in economic offshoots. Of course, the Family needs an enemy to fight, but that's easy. After centuries of indoctrination the world is so divided up by religion, skin color, nation, gender, culture, and region that all you need is a trickster like Donald Trump to frenzy up the masses and you're all set to go. When the world war is finally constructed, trillions of dollars are surreptitiously injected into the economy at the same that all the strong, angry young people are ripped from the bosom of their families and sent off to be culled in what we are now beginning to see is a historically repeated process of crisis management and population control.

Problem solved.

Of course, you can see the problem here. Cyclical global war[83] means permanent anguish and suffering for the majority of people on this earth. And while the Family

---

[83] For those too young to know, George Orwell covered most of the content covered in this essay in his classic book *1984*. In that book George Orwell painted a picture of a future totalitarian dystopia where the Family was in total control, and where they used perception sanitation, indoctrination, distraction, global war, and brutal psychological torture and repression, to control the people. The book 1984 is the source of the Hollywood fetish with the number "101," which you often see plastered on entranceways in Hollywood films. The book is well worth the read. See https://en.wikipedia.org/wiki/Nineteen_Eighty-Four.

might want to say to themselves, "what doesn't kill you makes you stronger," and while they may also want to say that all this suffering and anguish is just part of the "divine lesson plan," really none of the anguish and suffering is necessary. It is all avoidable and everybody could live happily ever after if we all got together and ended their regime of accumulation. It is that simple.

So the question remains, what are we going to do?

Well, I personally do not recommend you sit around and do nothing. Even if we ignore all the death, suffering, and war, and even if by some miracle the Family does manage to solve our global economic crisis by re-monetizing the global economy, we are rapidly reaching a planetary wall. If we do not fix the numerous ecological, psychological, political, and social distortions that are caused by the lunatic fringe leading this lunatic economic system, humanity probably won't survive to do it again. The ecosphere will collapse (see next section) and be unable to maintain human life, the "experiment" will be reset (so to speak), and those that survive will be thrown back to the dark ages. You have to remember, we are not using sticks and stones any more. With the type of military/media technology that can be deployed these days, and with the global interconnectedness that fuses the entire planet, billions could suffer and die.

As I have also said, I also do not recommend guillotines and violence. We may not like what the Family has been doing to the planet, but as I will speak about in more detail below, violence begets violence, always. If you solve problems with violence, vengeance, and oppression, then violent, oppressive, and vengeful people move in to take up the emptied spaces. Once they are in control, the System gets rebuilt and the cycle continues again. Therefore, it would be best if we did not setup the conditions for our own downfall. So once again the question remains, what are you (what are we) going to do?

THE SOLUTION

EDUCATION

I can think of a few things that might contribute towards a solution to the problem. The first thing we need to do, once we are clear on the issues and the problems, is educate others about the true nature of money and the true reality of accumulation and debt. A clear and precise understanding of the problem (i.e. accumulation of abstracted labor causes greed, economic distortion, and eventually global catastrophe) is a necessary precursor to rapid global change. Without a widespread understanding of the problem, it will be impossible to unify the people. Without a grounded and precise understanding, people will hem and haw, succumb to misdirection, perception sanitation, and indoctrination, misidentify themselves, misunderstand their true interests, misconstrue the situation, and otherwise fail to develop the focus and direction needed to come up with rapid solutions. Therefore, education, precision, and clarity are required.

As we are educating the population about the true nature of money and the economy we also have to link that understanding to the entire set of social, environmental, economic, psychological, and political problems we face. From ruined psychology through ruined economies and even ruined lives, the ruin brought by the System is, for many, total. Finding ways to link the financial truth of money, accumulation, and debt with the accumulating social, psychological, emotional, economic, political, and life catastrophes is a critical strategy. It is this linkage, made to touch as many life spheres as possible, that will provide the motivation to transform the planet.

I should note at this point, educating the population may be a bit easier to do than we first imagine. A lot of excellent work is being carried out by documentary film makers, bloggers, authors, educators, etc. Couple all that work with the potential of social media to disseminate information and you have an explosive situation. It wouldn't take much to make this sort of financial expose go viral. Many people these days know there is a problem, but these people are not altogether clear about just what the problem is. What's missing at this point is simple clarity. With clarity, those working to educate could refine, ramp up, and overdrive their educational efforts. With clarity, many more people could be educated and convinced. The solution to the global crisis isn't that hard to envisage after all. With clarity all those people who currently have no clue, who are indoctrinated, or who sit on the fence swinging back and forth (in various degrees of bewilderment and/or confusion) from one family solution (i.e. Republican/Conservative) to another (Liberal/NDP) without ever realizing that both sides are employed by the Family, could be moved to enlightenment and even action. And we shouldn't be discouraged by resistance from the Family. As we'll see below, cracks in the Family's resolve are appearing and these cracks will grow wider as the various psychological, emotional, economic, and even spiritual crisis impact their own members more and more.

Finally, for emphasis, I'm going to say again what I said above, and what I will repeat again below. Any solutions that we come up with will have to be rooted in clear perception of actual reality. Angry, dismissive, paranoid, delusional, confused statements, along with unclear presentation and calls for violence and punishment, will undermine the message. Efforts to educate the population must be framed by messages of unity and oneness. Education that divides us in any way supports the System. As we will see below, if you play the old energy games and invoke infidels, devils, demons, psychopaths, and evil invisible lizards,[84] you're not part of the solution, you are part of the problem (and in fact you may even be a paid *agent provocateur* of the Family). If you divide, you are creating enemies and perpetuating old energy patterns. It is OK to be angry and OK to expect accountability, but global transformation will not come on the heels of hatred and violence, period.

As a final note, and in order to help out with the program of education that we must all undertake, I am releasing this book for free as an eBook. Feel free to redistribute, excerpt, and otherwise use this book, which is designed to bring clarity and help people rapidly enlighten and connect the dots, in your educational efforts so long as you do not profit from the resale. If your intent is to profit, please contact me for permission. Also, if you are a media expert, animator, or filmmaker and would like to help create alternative media representations of the materials in this book, contact me.

---

[84] It might sound bizarre, but there are "spiritual" writers who demonize the .01 percent by invoking shape shifting, world-colonizing, alien lizards. This is a process of dehumanizing that can be likened to the Nazi process of dehumanizing Jews to make their "final solution" more palatable. When you dehumanize groups of people, you make violence against them easier.

DEBT JUBILEE

The second thing you can do to take steps towards a solution is get behind the notion of a **debt jubilee**. A debt jubilee is an event, first mentioned in biblical references, where debt is repudiated (i.e. forgiven and dismissed) outright. If we are going to fix the world, the world needs an immediate and global debt jubilee where all debt is forgiven because, as we have seen, debt is the problem. There is no reason not to do it because there is no good debt. Debt is the result of unfair accumulation practices, debt starves the economy, and debt eventually leads to horrific financial crisis; therefore, there is no ethical, financial, or social reason to hang onto existing debt. In order to truly reset the economy and change the world, debt has to be wiped out.

If this is the first time you are hearing about a debt jubilee, the suggestion may sound unworkable, even bizarre, but it is not, and many others are suggesting it as well. Erik Kain in *Forbes* Magazine suggests just this thing,[85] and he is not the only one.[86] People are aware of the problem, and people are already suggesting this as the solution. What is missing is global political will and global political pressure. You can help build up global will and political pressure by educating friends and family about the true nature of the problem, and by getting behind the notion of a debt jubilee. It can be done, and it needs to be done, fast. When the

---

[85] Erik Kain, "Could a Debt Jubilee Help Kickstart the American Economy?," *Forbes* (2011).

[86] See for example the *Jubilee Debt Campaign* at http://jubileedebt.org.uk/

über-crises hits, we need to be in an educated and willing position to make the necessary changes, otherwise a lot of people are going to suffer and die unnecessarily.

ECONOMIC REVOLUTION

Speaking of necessary changes, the **third thing** we can do to solve the problem, and even take a step towards utopia, is eliminate accumulation based economies. The primary reason we want to do this is to end the cycle of debt, recession, and collapse; but, there are environmental and ecological reasons as well. Economies where accumulation is encouraged develop massive productive and ethical distortions, and destroy the environment as a consequence of these distortions. Products are made to obsolesce. Marketing drives frenzied and wasteful production and consumption.[87] Useless and cheap inventions are pimped with no concern for children who labor as slaves in factories. The social, environmental, and psychological costs are ignored. Finally, bizarre distortions (like the selling of clean air to a polluted China) develop and exacerbate the problem.[88] The drive to accumulate money

---

[87] A particularly distasteful example of frenzied and wasteful production and consumption is the fast fashion industry. See the documentary film on fashion entitled *The True Cost* for details. http://www.sociology.org/film/true-cost/

[88] A Canadian company is selling clean mountain air to the poor people of China who are under, because of the frenzied pace of economic development and their desire to be more like the West, a toxic cloud of smog. Not only is this morally and ethically ridiculous, but it just contributes to environmental disaster. The resources taken up by the bottles (which would very likely be made in China) and the environmental costs of shipping bottles

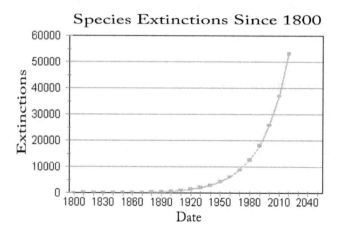

Species Extinctions Since 1800

undermines the biosphere and threatens life on the planet, and the situation is dire and getting worse. It is so bad that the extinction of life has reached the point of vertical takeoff! I believe the graphic above speaks for itself.[89] If this continues for even a few years longer, the biosphere of the planet is going to be wrecked and Earth will be unable to sustain human life at its current levels, if at all. And frankly, when the point of global mass extinction arrives, money isn't going to save you. If the food chain collapses and the planet's ecological system crashes, all the cash dollars in the world are not going to save you from the starving,

---

back to China where they were probably produced, make the actual practice fundamentally absurd. Yet in a Capitalist economy where accumulation is the goal, such a practice is not only possible, it is encouraged. It is this sort of thing that will end human life on this planet if we don't smarten up right now.

[89] The graphic is stolen from the page Anonymous, "Species Extinction and Human Population," http://www.whole-systems.org/extinctions.html.

desperate, hordes. You and your family are going to suffer and die just like everybody else. There is no dispensation available for higher social classes, and no special grace bestowed on the worthy by God. If this earth ship goes down, we all go down with it.

CONSCIOUSNESS AND VALUES

Besides educating the population, eliminating debt, and outlawing accumulation (or at least strictly controlling it), the **fourth thing** we can all do is change our values and priorities on a global scale. Education, a debt jubilee, and global economic change will not stick unless also accompanied by a fundamental change in values, rooted in an expansion of our individual and collective consciousness. Indeed, and arguably, people won't be motivated to educate themselves, forgive debt, or change the economy without some sort of fundamental revision in values. In this regard we need to de-emphasize materialism and emphasize human, even spiritual, values. We need empathic connection to each other and the planet. We need human contact, human service, human enlightenment, and human economies. Instead of spending tens of thousands of dollars of labor a year on cars, clothes, smart-phones,[90] and other useless accoutrements of ascending human misery, we need to

---

[90] Yes, smartphones are making you miserable. According to one recent study of students, the more you use your cell phone, the more miserable you are. Andrew Lepp, Jacob E. Barkley, and Aryn C. Karpinski, "The Relationship between Cell Phone Use, Academic Performance, Anxiety, and Satisfaction with Life in College Students," *Computers in Human Behavior* 31 (2014).

develop an authentic human society and an authentic human service economy that is aligned with our most authentic inner (species/divine) being. To reduce an incredibly long soundbite about our human/spiritual nature into a miniscule soundbite, we need to stop making our living in ways that destroy ourselves and this world, and start living our lives making a living in ways that represent who we truly are inside. In other words, we need more healers, therapists, life coaches, gardeners, interior designers, doctors, nurses, teachers, artists, musicians, entertainers, educators, and so on, (what I would call **new energy** jobs and services) and less of the jobs that destroy our psyches and obliterate our environments (what I would call **old energy** jobs and services).[91] Not that we won't still need or enjoy material things, but even science says we can do with a lot less materialism and a lot more human service, contact, and healing. There is no scientific evidence to suggest that having "things" makes us happy. Indeed, science points to precisely the opposite

---

[91] Just to be clear, I'm not suggesting we throw millions of people out of work. People will need to be transitioned from old energy jobs into new energy jobs in a way that doesn't disrupt, but instead improves, their life. That is difficult, but not impossible. A debt jubilee, including a jubilee on mortgages and other forms of consumer debt, that frees up global resources, the provision of free post-secondary education, and the expansion of the healing professions, will all support a gentle and compassionate transition to new energy economies.

conclusion, that excessive materialism makes us miserable.[92] So really, there is no excuse.

HOSTILE ENVIRONMENTS

Of course, it is one thing to say that we, as a species, need to change our values and priorities, but it is another thing to accomplish it at the scale required because there are a lot of challenges to raising consciousness and achieving authentic value change. One such challenge is a **hostile environment.** We live in a world that lives and breathes *accumulation. You do not have to go very far to hear* hymns and psalms to the capitalist way. Many people (including members of our own families) continue to tout the benefits of modern accumulation economies while blithely ignoring the apocalyptic downside.[93] Those who are

---

[92] For a fascinating, if dated, summary see Tori Deangelis, "Consumerism and Its Discontents," *Monitor on Psychology* 35, no. 6 (2004).

[93] Though to be sure, what with record temperatures, record flooding, record tornadoes, record droughts, record number of refugees, and record violence, it is increasingly difficult to ignore the "apocalyptic downside," According to one Canadian Broadcasting Corporation (CBC) reporter, "The number of people forcibly displaced worldwide is likely to have 'far surpassed' a record 60 million this year..."

If that number doesn't cause you anxiety and concern, let me put it in context for you. The number represents an astonishing one in every 122 humans! According to one UN report, we have entered into an "age of unprecedented mass displacement" And note that Sam's article points to numbers at the end of 2014! Surely the numbers now are even more apocalyptic than before.

critical of the System and the Family often feel the ire, even the wrath, of those who consciously or unconsciously defend the System. And it has only gotten worse in recent years where a saturated media universe provides on-going distraction, diversion, indoctrination, and ideology. Even if people do find something to plant their roots into, and even when they achieve some sort of alternative mind and life space, unsupportive, oppressive, and even violent environments often make it impossible to maintain progress and direction. On this world, and with the modern World Wide Web in place, it is very easy to see the truth; but hostile environments make it equally easy for the dead to oppress the living and for the blind to shut down and turn around those who achieved even minimal advances in sight.

Unfortunately, I can offer no easy advice to overcome hostile environments. People can experience hostile environments in several social locations, in their intimate relationships, families, work, friendship circles, schools, and so on. What's more, there are many variations in intensity and application of hostility. For some it is severe physical hostility, for others light emotional violence. Some experience punitive economic hostility while others experience passive aggressive, humor based psychological violence. Given the variety of hostility we face, it is difficult

---

For more see Stephanie Nebehay, "Refugee Numbers at Record Levels Globally, According to the Un," CBC, http://www.cbc.ca/news/world/un-refugee-estimates-2015-1.3371047; Sam Jones, "One in Every 122 People Is Displaced by War, Violence and Persecution, Says Un " *The Gaurdian*, June 2015.

to give general advice. What is worse, fixing these environments, while possible to do quickly if people are open, can often take years to accomplish when people resist. If you do face one of these environments (and all of us do to one extent or another) but are committed to forward change you have, assuming you are not living in a country with an oppressive political or economic regime, three choices. You can get out immediately and focus on yourself; you can stay and build strict boundaries that prevent violence and abuse; or you can commit to what may very well be difficult and long-term therapy and struggle to "save" the people around you who are imposing their toxic hostilities. What you do is up to you, and whatever you do it should be based on a careful and reasonable evaluation of the situation. If you choose option three and decide to stay, consistent and persistent efforts to *educate,* and gentle admonishment to seek healing, are a necessary first step towards breaking down resistance and opening up minds.

CORRUPTED ARCHETYPES AND IDEOLOGY

A hostile environment is not the only thing that makes value change difficult. Another challenge is there aren't any real spiritual, religious, or scientific alternatives. There appear to be a lot of alternatives, but the appearance is an illusion. In my opinion, all extant religious, humanistic, philosophical, and/or spiritual perspectives contain core ideological elements (what I would call archetypal seeds) that support the Family's System. That is, most understandings of the world, no matter how "alternative" or revolutionary they might feel, simply feed you back into the System by creating systems of thinking and behaving that support rather than undermine regimes of accumulation. Secular notions of evolution from apes, spiritual/religious notions of good versus evil, new age notions of "life lessons," even canonical understandings of God and human nature do nothing but prepare you for mental and physical slavery. In this context, replacing your current value system (e.g., shifting from Catholicism to Buddhism, or Buddhism to secular humanism) might look like a progressive alternative, but often it is simply more of the same old energy nonsense wrapped up in a new set of clothing.

Buddhism is a great example here. People with progressive spiritual awakenings often gravitate out of their traditional religious backgrounds towards Buddhism because they feel that Buddhism offers more aligned and authentic conceptualizations and practices. I have read the Buddha and while there is much wisdom and insight in his words, he (or perhaps the people who transcribed, translated, and/or interpreted his words) is also a product of the System, which he represented to a certain extent. According to legend, Buddha was the son of a rich man. It is said that he had three palaces built just for him that he could occupy on a seasonal basis. Given the Buddha's clear privileges, there is no arguing with the next statement: Buddha was a member of the Family, and this impacted his spirituality and spiritual teaching.

You can see the impact of his privilege on his spirituality and spiritual teaching right out of the gate. Buddha was isolated from the world as a child, but when he finally went out to see, the first thing he noticed was all the suffering that surrounded him. For all the spiritual wisdom gleaned from his mystical experiences under the Bodhi tree,

Buddha never made a connection between the suffering of the people and the privilege of his family. That is, his explanation for suffering was not exploitation or his family's accumulation. He found a way to blame the people. He said suffering was caused by "attachment" and if the people wanted to overcome their suffering, they should simply overcome their attachment. If people were not so attached to things (which his family accumulated from them), to their loved ones, and even to their own life (all things that, as we have seen, are put in grave jeopardy by accumulation regimes), said the Buddha, they would not suffer so much! Thus it is not that accumulation is draining the economy and putting you in jeopardy, it is your "attachment" to things that you cannot have (i.e. health, wealth, and even a place to live) that is the problem. What a convenient (for the Family) thing for him to say! With a simple gesture of his mystical spiritual wisdom Buddha neatly displaces a critical understanding of his family's accumulation with an ideological distraction that makes the people's attachment the source of the pain.

If you are a little shocked by this revelation, don't be. Given Buddha's privileged background, is it really that surprising to think that Buddha would say these things? Is it really that shocking to find the Buddha doing what members of the Family always do, utter justification and excuse?

Of course, Buddha may not have intended his statements to root centuries of spiritual ideology. Buddha may simply have been motivated by an unconscious desire to *not* accuse his parents and family, whom he was (ironically) probably quite attached to, of great evil. Regardless, it is the same. For all his other wonderful insight and advice, his core philosophy of non-attachment is not a tidbit of spiritual wisdom, it is a convenient justification for the suffering caused by his Family's accumulation. His wisdom is not about spirituality, enlightenment, ascension, or anything like that; it is simple justification that shifts attention and blame away from the wealthy and privileged and toward the battered and impoverished. It is a classic "blame the victim" strategy and it has been effective as such for thousands of years.

Buddhism is not the only spirituality with elements supportive of the Family in it. Christianity, Judaism, Hinduism, and all of the major world traditions contain elements of ideology that support inequality, privilege, power over others, and accumulation regimes. Hindu scriptures, for example, provide remarkably powerful and pertinacious justifications for privilege and accumulation. The Laws of Manu,[94] part of Hindu sacred texts known as the Dharma sutras, open with a blatant justification of social class (not to mention a total disrespect for women). During the middle ages, Catholic priests told the peasants that the King was God's vicegerent (i.e. head of state) on Earth, and that obeying the King (i.e. obeying the head of the Family) was tantamount to obeying God.[95] Priests also justified social hierarchy by saying that peasants were

---

[94] If you have the patience, you can read the Laws for yourself. George Bühler, "The Laws of Manu," Sacred-Texts.com, http://www.sacred-texts.com/hin/manu.htm.

[95] The Wikipedia page on the Divine Right of Kings does a decent job of explaining the concept. Wikipedia, "Divine Right of Kings," Wikipedia, https://en.wikipedia.org/wiki/Divine_right_of_kings.

peasants because God wanted it that way! In this way, Christianity served the Family by providing ideological support for their brutal accumulation regimes.

Speaking of "blame the victim" strategies, science can be just as bad as Christianity, Buddhism, Hinduism, or any other corrupted spiritual perspective. To be as blunt as possible, science is an ideology[96] and like all ideologies, science too can be used as a justification for accumulation. A good example here is the "alpha male" notion that nature organizes its social fabric into a pyramid of "strong crush the weak" domination. According to this mythology alpha males, because of their "natural" superiority and strength, rise to the top where they "dominate" their respective spheres. Domination of others is thus transformed from a psychopathy to a "natural" and acceptable behavior.

The problem with viewing alpha male behavior as a "natural" behavior is that it is simply a wrong idea. It is, to be perfectly blunt, pure ideology. The term itself was originally popularized by Dr. David L. Mech, a biologist and *the* global authority on wolf behavior. He used the term way back in the day because he was relying on a single piece of fundamentally flawed research conducted by a fellow by the name of Rudolph Schenkel. In order to study wolf behavior, Schenkel took a bunch of "individual wolves from various zoos and placed them together in their own

---

[96] See for example Paul Feyerabend, "How to Defend Society against Science," *Radical Philosophy*, no. 11 (1975).

captive colony."[97] Apparently, says Mech, "when one puts a random group of any species together artificially, these animals will 'naturally' compete with each other and eventually form a type of dominance hierarchy."[98] But as noted, the experiment was flawed, and as Mech has now admitted,[99] there is nothing "natural" about alpha behavior at all. As he says:

> ...most wolves who lead packs achieved their position simply by mating and producing pups, which then became their pack. In other words they are merely breeders, or <u>parents</u>, and that's all we call them today, the "breeding male," "breeding female," "male parent," "female parent," the "adult male," or "adult female." In the rare packs that include more than one breeding animal, the "dominant breeder" can be called that, and any breeding daughter can be called a "subordinate breeder."[100]

In other words, in their natural environment, male and female wolves act like responsible, attached parents. However, if you rip a bunch of young males from their families and confine them together between four prison walls (which scientists euphemistically call a "laboratory"), they "naturally" compete and form a dominance hierarchy.

---

[97] David Mech, "Whatever Happened to the Term Alpha Wolf," *International Wolf,* Winter 2008.: emphasis added

[98] Ibid., 6. scare quotes added

[99] David L. Mech, "Leadership in Wolf, *Canus Lupus,* Packs," *Canadian Field-Naturalist* 11, no. 2 (2000).

[100] David Mech, "Outmoded Notion of the Alpha Wolf," Dave Mech, http://www.davemech.org/news.html. emphasis added.

It is wonderful that Mech has retracted his fallacious statements about alpha males. He made an honest mistake and when he realized his mistake, he immediately moved to retract it. However, there are two problems with Mech's retraction. On the one hand, the Family is *not* letting him retract his fallacious statements. Despite his "numerous pleas to his publisher to stop publishing it,"[101] they won't let him! The publisher, a big university press probably run by hand-picked members of the Family, won't even let him revise the book! They just keep printing it with the now debunked alpha male ideology preserved as is. If you have naïve faith in science, then the refusal of the press to allow him to revise his own work becomes inexplicable. You would assume that a university press (a part of the Institute) would be primarily concerned with the truth of the science and would thus let him revise and recant as necessary, but they do not. Why? The actions of his publisher only become sensible when you realize that the chief executives of the press are acting in the interests of the Family. They continue to publish debunked ideology about "alpha males" precisely because this idea of "natural dominance" is a powerful plank in ideological justifications for their accumulation activities.

It is simple really. If you look at members of the Family and ask "why are they at the top?" the answer isn't that they engage in unfair and secretive practices of accumulation, the answer is that they are "strong alphas." If you ask why members of the Family engage in aggressive acts of domination and control, the answer isn't that they are

---

[101] You can read Mech's own words on the refusal of his press to let him retract at ibid.

135

emotionally disturbed in some fashion (perhaps because they have been separated from their families and placed into the confines of male-only "lodges") the answer is that they are expressing their "natural" evolutionary propensities. By suggesting that "alphas" are acting "naturally," Mech invokes the full authority of science (just like a priest may invoke the full authority of the bible, or God) in order to provide an easy ideological cover for arguably toxic patterns of behavior. This is exactly what the Buddha did when he invoked the full weight of his spiritual/mystical connection to justify his family's privilege, and it is exactly what so many others do when they come with their excuses and justifications. It is hard to make an argument against accumulation regimes or the toxic behavior of emotionally disturbed alpha males in their toxic corporate environments when their actions are conceived of as "natural," inevitable, and even God given.

The other problem with Mech's retraction, besides the fact that a university press won't let him retract it, is that he doesn't go far enough in his critical analysis. He says, and I quote, "when one puts a **random group** of any species together artificially, these animals will 'naturally' compete with each other." Mech suggests that it is "natural" for wolves to compete in the "unnatural" environment of the lab, but there are two problems with that statement. On the one hand, Mech is not accurately reflecting actual events. Wolves were not simply "put together," they were ripped from their natural environments, stolen from their families, and deposited in unnatural environments where they were observed in an unnatural fashion. On the other hand, the wolves were not developing "natural" dominance behaviors, as apologists might suggest, they were acting in disturbed and violent ways. To be as precise as possible, there is nothing natural about a zoo or a laboratory and so there is nothing natural about the wolf behavior that emerges in those toxic environments. What Schenkel really did, and what Mech should really be saying, is if you rip wolves from their natural environment and family and throw them together into a confined and unpleasant space, they become emotionally disturbed and violent. In other words, when you lock wolves up, they develop a violent psychopathology. It is not "natural" competitive behavior at all; it is unnatural emotional disturbance. This makes total sense. Wolves are social and like all social animals if you lock them away from their friends and family they become quite disturbed.

As you can see, there is a different way of viewing the behavior of confined male wolves, one that does not provide ideological support for the toxic behavior of the Family. Seen in this alternative light, alpha male behavior is not normal, it is pathology that emerges from the oppressive actions of scientists callously studying wolf behavior with no regard for wolf feelings. In other words, alpha males are not the strong and tough CEOs of the natural world, they are emotionally disturbed prisoners of a system they have no control over. We could even suggest, as I have done above, and as others are starting to do, that it (i.e. alpha behavior) is pure criminal psychopathology. Jon Ronson wrote a book tagging corporate and media elites as pure psychopaths.[102] He makes the argument that many of the activities that are considered "natural" in our

---

[102] Jon Ronson, *The Psychopath Test: A Journey through the Madness Industry*(United Saates: Picador, 2011).

modern capitalist accumulation regimes are in fact pure psychopathy, and given some of the actions that corporations have taken over the last century or so,[103] it is hard not to agree. It may seem like a strong statement to some, but as we see with the ideology of the "alpha wolf," it doesn't take much of a shift to see "alpha behavior" in a totally different light.

NEW WAYS OF THINKING

As you can probably imagine, hostile environments and corrupted ideologies like the "alpha male" ideology are big obstacles to value change because they normalize the toxic behaviors of the Family. A **third challenge** to value change is the challenge of coming up with new ways of looking at things, ways that do not intentionally or unintentionally feed you back into the System. This can be a big challenge on its own (i.e. it takes a lot of time and intellectual effort to rethink archetypes and ideas), but it is even harder when you consider the fact that even the most progressive ways of rethinking have failed to lead to significant and permanent value change. For example, the political and economic philosophy of Karl Marx was clearly and

---

[103] For some comments on the "global corporate crime wave," see Jeffrey D. Sachs, "The Global Economy's Corporate Crime Wave," *Project Syndicate* 2011.

If you are interested in learning more, there are many sites that catalog corporate psychopathy. See for examples *The Global Exchange's* page on the top 10 corporate criminals (http://www.globalexchange.org/corporateHRviolators). Just search for the key phrase "corporate crimes," "global corporate crimes," or something similar.

unambiguously intended to bring an end to the Family's destructive regime of accumulation. Marx even thought that with these new ideas we could bring about global utopia!

Unfortunately, Marx's ideas and his effort failed to lead to global transformation. Despite Marx's progressive intent, his ideas were transformed to the psychopathic governmental expressions of Joseph Stalin and the Russian communist party. But you should know, what happened in Russia was as far from Marx's utopian vision of communism as ancient barter is from modern electronic finance. Karl Marx, and others who spoke of ending the Family's Regime, were clear that under a communist utopia, **there would be no governments**(!) **and no accumulation**. As Busky notes:

> ...communism meant a classless and stateless society **without government** or organs for law and order; for there would be no one left to repress or to keep in check, and no compensation would have to be paid for work. Communism would mean free distribution of goods and services. The communist slogan, "From each according to his ability to each according to his needs"... would then rule.[104]

I imagine the notion that Marx was calling for *no state* and *no accumulation* is going to come as a big surprise to many fooled by the Family's justification, excuse, and ideologically based dismissal of his work, but Karl Marx felt that once accumulation was outlawed, the state would simply "wither away." This is because Marx saw the state

---

[104] Donald F Busky, *Democratic Socialism: A Global Survey* (Westport, CT: Praeger, 2000), 4.: emphasis added

as merely a tool used by the people at the top of the hill, (whom he called the **bourgeoisie,** but what these days we would call the .01 percent) to facilitate accumulation from the people at the bottom (whom he called the **proletariat,** but what these days we would call the ninety nine percent). Marx felt that the state created the laws, enacted the legislation, and controlled the police and military forces, mostly on behalf of the Family. In other words, the state supported the **Regime**. In other, words, the state (like the media, the elite universities, the K-12 system, the biggest corporations, or the parents who uncritically socialize their children with myths like the alpha male) was merely an obedient and compliant arm of the Family.[105] Marx felt that once the Regime was gone, and once the people were no longer subject to the oppression, repression, exploitation,

---

[105] That the state is an obedient and compliant arm of the Family is very clear in U.S. politics where the cost of winning the presidential election is staggering, and where only the very rich have a chance of winning. In other words, in the United States, and of course in most other countries around the world, only Family members get elected.

A fortune magazine article suggests that the cost of winning a U.S. election runs in the tens of millions, but that is a suspiciously low estimate. An uncredited writer writing in the *Bangor Daily News* suggests, and I believe him, that it costs between $500 million and 1 billion dollars to win a U.S. election! In the United States, like in a lot of other places in the world, anybody can run, but you can only win if you are backed by big money. See Tory Newmyer, "This Is What It Costs to Run for President," *Fortune*, March 28 2015; "How Much Does It Cost to Run for President?," *Bangor Daily News* 2015.

and (what I would call) **toxic socialization**[106] meted upon them by the (witting or unwitting) agents of the Regime, there would be no need for a state, a police force, jails, or any of the other oppressive and violent accoutrements of modern accumulation regimes.

Marx developed his analysis of the Family's regime in a three volume expose of the Family's accumulation operation entitled *Das Capital* (or just *Capital,* in English).[107] The three volume tome was complemented by his *Communist Manifesto.* In the Communist Manifesto, Marx summarized his analysis and called out to the people to rise up, overthrow the Family, and replace their oppressive regime of accumulation with a utopian alternative. I have to say, Marx was no slacker. Marx developed an entirely new way of thinking about the world, provided that to the People, and then encouraged them to use their new found economic enlightenment to demolish the Regime.[108] The problem was that Karl Marx's

---

[106] **Toxic Socialization** is a socialization process specifically designed to fracture attachments, undermine Self Esteem, destroy ego boundaries, and disable the body's ability to contain higher levels of Consciousness. For more details, view the SpiritWiki page.

http://spiritwiki.lightningpath.org/Toxic_Socialization

[107] Karl Marx, *Das Capital: A Critique of Political Economy*, trans. Samuel Moore and Edward Aveling, Three vols., vol. One(Russia: Progress Publishers, 1867).

[108]I encourage you to spend a few moments reading Marx's Communist Manifesto. Karl Marx and Frederick Engels, *The Communist Manifesto*(Oxford: Oxford Paperbacks, 2008). I believe you will find it easier to understand now that you have the

progressive analysis and new way of thinking did not trigger the end of the Regime. Instead it spawned one of the most brutal and repressive regimes in the history of accumulation, communist Russia. In communist Russia, and in other "communist states,"[109] accumulation still occurred, it just went into the hands of state officials instead of corporate individuals. Same boss, different name.

What happened to the otherwise progressive dreams of Karl Marx and why did Russia turn into just another Family stronghold? It is because Marx for all his painstaking and detailed economic analysis, missed something important. Eugene Ruyle, commenting about the failure of the communist revolution, says that if we are to be successful in eliminating regimes of accumulation we have to remove the "basis of class society." If we do not remove the basis of class society, says Ruyle, regimes of accumulation simply re-emerge. It is worth quoting Ruyle at length:

> If the struggle for a socialist society is to be successful, it is essential to have a sharper vision of that future society. In this connection, I would argue that the features usually proclaimed as indicating socialism, such as planning and social ownership of the means of production, are inadequate, for, as the Soviet example indicates, exploitation can re-emerge even in such a system. Rather, the diagnostic feature is the

---

foundation provided by this *Rocket Guide.* You can find it freely available online by searching "Communist Manifesto."

[109] At this point you will realize the dark irony of the phrase "communist state" since, according to Marx and others, communism would not have a state!

elimination of exploitation in any form. When this basis of class society is removed, the attendant evils will also be removed, and not until. It is essential that Marxists remain aware of this problem and create ways and means to block the reemergence of exploitation during revolutionary periods, and following them.[110]

In the quotation above, Ruyle suggests that the basis of class society is *exploitation*, and that is certainly true. If we do not remove the basis of exploitation, then exploitation simply re-emerges after the revolution when exploitative, violent, and even psychopathic people, who are the most likely to want to move into positions of power over others, move in and setup their kakistocracy all over again.

At this point the obvious question is, what is the basis of exploitation. The answer to that is simple. *The basis of exploitation is violence.* You see, exploiting another person is a fundamentally violent act. It may not always be overtly violent, but it is violent all the same. If you take money from some "loser" in the stock market, if you squeeze workers' wages until they can no longer support their life, if you buy a corporation and then fire all the workers to improve a bottom line, if you rape Gaia of her resources and dump her with toxic slime (all common acts), you are engaging in violence. Every act of exploitation that there ever was is a violent act. Therefore, violence is

---

[110] Eugene E. Ruyle, "Mode of Production and Mode of Exploitation: The Mechanical and the Dialectical," *Dialectical Anthropology* 1, no. 1 (1975).

the basis for exploitation. If we all just stopped acting violently, exploitation would disappear overnight.

So, how do we stop acting violently? That is easy. We stop violence when we stop giving ourselves excuses for it. As strange as it may sound, we (and by "we" I mean humans) have many excuses to justify our violent behavior. We assault our kids and tell ourselves "Spare the rod." We watch boys beat each other in the playground and say "It's just boys being boys." We let girls attack each other in orgies of social violence. We attack another nation and invoke God's will or Allah's way to justify it. We kill and we excuse ourselves of the crime because we tell ourselves our victims are evil (or they have given into the "dark side", or whatever). We beat, colonize, execute, revolt, and even damn ourselves to hell all on a set of excuses that we give ourselves to make the violence we engage in right. Truly, if we would stop giving ourselves excuses and just say "violence is never a good thing," we would all stop engaging in violence. Of course, it wouldn't happen overnight. Given how many people have been hurt by the physical, psychological, emotional, and spiritual violence of this planet, a lot of healing has to occur. But the violence ends, and the work starts, when we stop giving ourselves excuses.

OLD AND NEW ENERGY ARCHETYPES

Of course, it is one thing to stop acting violently after we have stopped giving ourselves excuses, but it is quite another thing to actually stop giving ourselves excuses. Halting our excuses can be quite a challenge. The problem is that the excuses for violence that we give ourselves are supported by deeply embedded **archetypes** and ideas that we generally are not aware of, and that we *never examine*.

As I explain in my *Book of the Triumph of Spirit* series, archetypes are basically **big ideas** that answer **big questions**. Archetypes answer questions like "who are you" and "why are you here." As I explain, we (and by "we" I mean individuals and groups working in the interests of the Family) have developed many archetypes and ideas that justify and excuse all sorts of bad behavior. It is these archetypes that the Family have developed, these big answers to the big questions about human nature, God, consciousness, and even life purpose, that provide the fertile field for violence and exploitation. Therefore, if we want to stop violence, remove the basis of exploitation, and successfully change the world, *we have to change out all the archetypes and ideas that justify and excuse violence and replace them with ideas and archetypes that do not.*[111]

In order to help get us thinking about our archetypes and ideas in a critical way, I call ideas and archetypes that support hierarchy, control, elitism, and privilege **old energy archetypes**.[112] Old energy archetypes provide, in Ruyle's conception, the basis of exploitation. Old energy archetypes provide us with excuses and justification for

---

[111] This is not a particularly original insight. Karl Marx, and others, spent a considerable amount of time trying to change people's ideas and archetypes, in particular vis a vis *human nature.* His archetypal foundation for removing the basis of exploitation was the development of his notion of *species being* and his discussion of *alienation* from species being. See in particular Bertrell Ollman, *Alienation: Marx's Conception of Man in Capitalist Society*(Cambridge: Cambridge University Press, 1977). Unfortunately, Marx's presentation of *species being* was insufficient.

[112] http://spiritwiki.lightningpath.org/Old_Energy_Archetypes

violence, which in turn supports exploitation and violent accumulation. Old energy archetypes may be counterpoised to **new energy archetypes**.[113] New energy archetypes reject hierarchy, control, elitism, and privilege, and do not provide excuses nor support violence against others. New energy archetypes remove the basis of exploitation and provide a solid foundation for authentic spiritual and/or humanistic action in the world. It is new energy archetypes that we must all learn to think with.

None of us on the planet are taught to think very critically about archetypes and ideas and how these impact our thinking and behavior, but once they are pointed out they become quite easy to see. A couple of examples will have to suffice here. Our first example is the movie franchise Star Wars. Star Wars is the single biggest modern example of old energy archetypes that we have. That movie provides us with an archetypal image of the universe as a battlefield between the forces of "dark" and "light." In that movie we see the forces of light constantly putting down the forces of dark. There is incredible violence in the movie, but we never question the violence because the implicit and explicit message of the movie, the archetype that is seeded into our consciousness, is that it is OK to be violent if the other person is evil, bad, or someone who has "given in to the dark side." The message of the religion of Star Wars, just like the message of the religion of Christianity, is clear; there is a dark side and a light side and if you work for the "dark side" it is OK to put you down. The message is the same in all other traditional religions. From Catholicism to Hinduism, Buddhism to Islam, Freemasonry to

---

[113] http://spiritwiki.lightningpath.org/New_Energy_Archetypes

Lucasism.[114] If you work for the "dark side" it's a good thing to put you down.

---

[114] Interestingly, according to a Freemason by the name of Todd E. Reason, George Lucas dumps a lot of masonic imagery and symbolism into his movies. It is worth quoting Mr. Reason at length.

> I couldn't help but notice as I watched the *Star Wars* movies again how similar the ancient order of Jedi was to Freemasonry. I began to wonder if maybe George Lucas hadn't modelled that ancient Jedi order on the Craft. Once I started looking for it, I noticed how often terms like "apprentice" and "Master" and "Knight" had been used in the movies. And of course there's the Jedi Council that meets in the Temple--and they have a Grand Master, Yoda. A source of great wisdom, enlightenment and leadership. Sure enough, I wasn't the only person that had noticed it--do a Google search if you dare. The stark symbolism of darkness and light. The emphasis of staying on the more difficult enlightened path, and not being seduced by the dark side. The goal of becoming a better man. The idea of old mentors of the Craft helping apprentices learn traits and skills that enable them to be a force of good in the world. All very strangely Masonic.

I would not be surprised to find that George Lucas was the member of Freemasonry or one of the other secret boy's clubs that dot the spiritual landscape of our planet.

See Todd E. Reason, "Master Yoda: Freemason or Not?," Midnight Freemasons, www.midnightfreemasons.org/2012/05/master-yoda-freemason-or-not_16.html.

Freemasonry, which is a European based fraternal secret organization where wealthy and privileged members of the Family (and those who wannabe members) get together to hobnob and plan,[115] is another interesting case in point here. Like all other traditional religions, Freemasonry pimps the good versus evil archetype and uses that to excuse and justify the violent conditions of the world. They do so in the "checkboard" imagery that they use to indoctrinate new members. According to Freemasons, the checkboard is simply a representation of the "universal truth" that the cosmos is organized into opposing forces of black and white. For Freemasons and so many others, both good and evil are a necessary dialectical opposition, part of God's design or Nature's plan, part of a system of cosmic tutelage that helps us all grow and develop. As Lomas, a famous representative of the Freemason's faith, notes:

> These are the dualisms inherent in the physical world of which we are a part. Experience of these opposites is essential for human growth. Our existence consists of perpetual movement, like chessmen, from a white square to a black and from a black to a white. These moves continually test us and form our character; we grow as a result of our responses to both good and bad conditions. For how can we say that one class of experience is better

---

[115] For a detailed overview of Freemasonry, its origins, and how it functions to define and subsequently reproduce modern Family relations, see Mike Sosteric, "A Sociology of Tarot," *Canadian Journal of Sociology* 39, no. 3 (2014).

or worse than the other? Each is necessary and each complementary.[116]

For Freemasons,[117] bad isn't bad, it is just a cosmic opportunity to learn and grow. In this way the bad things of life, like the suffering, despair, and anguish caused by the Family's violent accumulation regime, are whisked away with a nefarious application of ideological sleight of hand.

It is noteworthy that Karl Marx pimped his own version of this "good versus evil" justification of violence and abuse, as did Hegel before him! They didn't call it good versus evil however. In an effort to make it sound more like scientific truth and less like the superstitious nonsense that it was, they called it "thesis" and "antithesis." For Marx and Hegel, it was not God Versus Satan, or Luke versus Darth, it was thesis versus antithesis. For Marx and Hegel, thesis and antithesis duked it out on a cosmic (for Hegel) and natural (for Marx) stage that, through the struggle that ensued, lead us all towards a higher "synthesis." Marx predicated the revolutionary success of the proletariat on the inevitable synthesis that would come from dialectical violence (euphemized as "struggle") between the capitalists (synthesis) and the proletariat (antithesis). Thus Marx, like Hegel, like a Catholic priest, like a Freemason, and like all good Star Wars geeks, put on what he thought were Jedi robes and

---

[116] Robert Lomas, *The Secret Science of Masonic Initiation* (San Francisco: Weiser, 2010), 27.

[117] And interestingly, you find this Masonic idea deeply embedded in so called *New Age* and *New Thought* spiritual alternatives.

provided standard rhetoric that justified, excused, and even encouraged violence against what he saw as the dark side. We can see this justification quite clearly in the words of Joseph Stalin who pinned the "dark side" on the bourgeoisie past and the light sight on the proletariat future. Notice as you read the passage below how similar Stalin's words are to the words of Freemason Lomas on the previous page. The only difference is that whereas Lomas refers to individual human growth, Stalin refers to collective political growth. It is the same ideology just aimed at a different aggregate level of human experience. Here are Stalin's words:

> ...dialectics holds that internal contradictions are inherent in all things and phenomena of nature, for they all have their negative and positive sides, a past and a future, something dying away and something developing; and that the struggle between these opposites, the struggle between the old and the new, between that which is dying away and that which is being born, between that which is disappearing and that which is developing, constitutes the internal content of the process of development...[118]

The similarity between the Masonic view, which is a view of social and economic elites, and the view of Marx, Engels, Lenin, and Stalin, is striking! Could it be that the "progressive" socialists of the world merely reproduced standard old energy excuses for violence and abuse? Could it be that the presence of these old energy justifications for

---

[118] J.V. Stalin, "Dialectical and Historical Materialsm," Marxists Internet Archive,
https://www.marxists.org/reference/archive/stalin/works/1938/09.htm.

violence and abuse allowed proto-capitalist "revisionists" to take over and turn back progress that may have been made towards achieving a stateless, accumulation-less, communist utopia.[119] I would argue, yes.

Anyway, I don't want to go into the details of the Hegelian or Marxian dialectic here. I just want to point out that for all the (sometimes) arrogant presupposition to be an authentic alternative to bourgeoisie metaphysics, the dialectical theory of history is nothing more than a gussied up version of an ancient archetypal delusion. This gussied up version preserved the "basis of exploitation" and provided the violent doorway through which Family members could subvert a utopian move.

Of course at this point you might be saying "so what." At this point you may actually be defending Jedi ideology, Masonic checkerboards, Christian metaphysics, or dialectical materialism as an actual, dyed in the wool, fact of our cosmic/natural reality. If you are defending this, I only have one thing to say to you and that is this: it is pure bullshit. The biggest lie of our century is the lie that the "experience of opposites" causes human growth. We do not grow or develop or strengthen as a result of our responses to both good and bad conditions. We are like flowers or any other living thing. We grow when we are nurtured in supportive, healthy, and non-toxic environments, but we weaken and die when the soil is sand, the water is insufficient, or some animal stomps all over us. As the esteemed American psychologist Abraham Maslow

---

[119] Bill Bland, "Stalin: The Myth and the Reality," Marxists Internet Archive, https://www.marxists.org/archive/bland/1999/x01/x01.htm.

pointed out decades ago, we grow when our needs are met,[120] and as has been made clear by a wealth of recent research on the profoundly negative outcomes of violence and neglect, we become damaged when we are stressed and assaulted. For example, one study among many finds that child abuse has long term negative emotional, psychological, and behavioral effects. As the authors of the study note, "Adolescents maltreated early in life were absent from school more than 1.5 as many days, were less likely to anticipate attending college compared with non-maltreated adolescents, and had levels of aggression, anxiety/depression, dissociation, posttraumatic stress disorder symptoms, social problems, thought problems, and social withdrawal that were on average more than three quarters of an SD higher than those of their non-maltreated counterparts. The findings held after controlling for family and child characteristics correlated with maltreatment."[121] Most important to note, children who exhibit negative effects engage in negative activities which draw sanction and further negative consequences. That is, children who have been abused at home act out, and this puts them at further risk from teachers, principals, and other authority figures

---

[120] A.H. Maslow, "A Theory of Human Motivation," *Psychological Review* 50, no. 4 (1943); A. H. Maslow, *Towards a Psychology of Being (2nd Edition)*(New York: Van Nostrand Reinhold Company, 1968); A.H. Maslow, *The Farther Reaches of Human Nature*(New York: Viking, 1971).

[121] J. E. Lansford et al., "A 12-Year Prospective Study of the Long-Term Effects of Early Child Physical Maltreatment on Psychological, Behavioral, and Academic Problems in Adolescence," *Archives of Pediatrics & Adolescent Medicine* 156, no. 8 (2002): 1072.

with whom they interact. A negative feedback loop is set up where negative impact accumulates for children. In the long run they suffer in profound and debilitating ways. Truly, there is nothing salutatory or beneficial about duking it out on the violent, dialectical, masonic, Christian checkboard of Jedi led toxicity, violence, and abuse.[122]

And note, it is not just abuse and violence that damages us. Poverty doesn't do us any good as well. "Low family income has been associated with delay or dysfunction in nearly all domains of children's development, including child behavior problems."[123] As Joan Luby points out, the experience of poverty, poverty which we have seen is caused by the Family's accumulation activities, means smaller brains!

> ...exposure to poverty during early childhood is associated with smaller white matter, cortical gray matter, and hippocampal and amygdala volumes measured at school age/early adolescence. These findings extend the substantial body of behavioral data demonstrating the deleterious effects of poverty

---

[122] For a summary of research on the negative impact of violence and abuse, see my SpiritWiki entry on Toxic Socialization. http://spiritwiki.lightningpath.org/Toxic_Socialization.

[123] Henrik D. Zachrisson and Eric Dearing, "Family Income Dynamics, Early Childhood Education and Care, and Early Child Behavior Problems in Norway," *Child Development* 86, no. 2 (2015): 425. See also Eric Dearing and Beck A. Taylor, "Home Improvements: Within-Family Associations between Income and the Quality of Children's Home Environments," *Journal of Applied Developmental Psychology* 28, no. 5-6 (2007).

on child developmental outcomes into the neurodevelopmental domain and are consistent with prior results.[124]

In other words, it is not a case of "what doesn't kill you makes you stronger", as the Freemasons and so many others might want to say to justify the bad behavior that harms us, it is a case of what doesn't kill you leaves a scar.

A lot of people who read this truth are going to be very upset by it, and rightly so. I was born poor and it put me at a major disadvantage in several ways. I am a white male however, so I am luckier than most; but even so, it has been a struggle. Poverty is abusive to our potential just as physical, emotional, mental, and spiritual violence are. There is no point in denying this fact and so there is no point in believing the religious indoctrination designed to get us to view adversity in a positive light. Instead, we should accept the truth and work to fix the problem. We should give up our excuses and work to end poverty, end toxic socialization, and provide a wealth of social, psychological, educational, and even spiritual supports to the people who have been victimized by the System.

But, I'm jumping ahead. We are discussing old and new energy archetypes and the point I am trying to make is that

---

[124] Luby et al., "The Effects of Poverty on Childhood Brain Development: The Mediating Effect of Caregiving and Stressful Life Events."

See also Yoshikawa, Aber, and Beardslee, "The Effects of Poverty on the Mental, Emotional, and Behavioral Health of Children and Youth: Implications for Prevention."

it is not a case of good versus evil, it is a case of old energy archetypes being exploited by those in power to turn us towards imperialism and violence towards the people who they define as "bad." When we believe the archetypal lie that we live in a universe of good and evil, then it is easy for Family members to exploit us and get us to act violently towards others. All they have to do is paint the "other" as evil and we pick up our guns and we shoot.

I realize at this point there may be a lot of objections to what I am saying. You look at organizations like Isis, or lunatics like Hitler, and you want to conclude there is great evil and that the only solution is a violent one. But you may want to consider this. The Germans who supported Adolph Hitler and joined his armies, and the Arabs and Muslims who join Isis, do not join up saying to themselves "I'm working for the dark side now." They say exactly what every other soldier says when he or she picks up a weapon and engages in violence. They say "the other guy is working for the dark side and I'm working to bring light, justice, and democracy." Isis sees America as evil and imperialistic just as the American's see Isis as violent, evil, barbarians. Both see themselves as on the side of right; both use violence to get their way; both are simply playing out the same old energy archetypal game implanted in their minds by the elites who control this planet's ideas and archetypes.

And it is the same with all conflicts!

Hitler's machine issued propaganda demonizing Jews and portraying them as greedy, evil, bankers who exploited the people, and raped women.[125] He did this because he knew that if he could convince the German people that Jews worked for the "dark side", then he could get his Aryan/Jedi's to act violently towards them. Hitler exploited this old energy archetype and was able to murder many people as a result. And it goes both ways. When the American government wanted to thrust American boys into war, they did exactly what Hitler did. They painted the Germans as vile and evil and they portrayed Hitler as an early version of Darth Vader. Of course, George Lucas did a much better job with the Darth Vader/Evil versus Luke Skywalker/Good duality than early media propagandists, but the result is the same. The common thread on both sides is the belief in good and evil, dark and light, and the justification this provides for violence. Both sides justify their violence by an appeal to the pernicious and perpetual archetype of light versus dark. And indeed, this is the way it always is. Every conqueror, psychopath, president, and prime minister in the history of the world has been able to manipulate the people into violence by invoking this ancient and nefarious archetype. It is our belief that we work for the light that justifies our violence against those we tag as the dark.

If you are still on the fence about this whole old energy good versus evil archetype thing, consider this. The actual archetype of good and evil, the view of the cosmos as a dialectical checkerboard, what J. Harold Ellens[126] calls the

---

[125] You can view some of the posters by searching for Internet images with the keywords "Nazi anti semitic propaganda posters"

[126] J. Harold Ellens, "Introduction: The Destructive Power of Religion," in *The Destructive Power of Religion: Violence in*

"Master Story," is traceable to a very specific historic location, specifically ancient Mesopotamian and Egyptian paganism.[127] From an ancient source of spiritual ideology, modern apocalyptic visions cosmic conflict between good and evil, and world ending violence emerge! It is worth quoting him at length.

> ...the Western religious traditions, which go back to the ancient Israelite religion of the Hebrew Bible, have internalized this violent metaphor of the cosmic contest between transcendental good and evil. It is an old pagan idea that derives from ancient Mesopotamian, Egyptian, and Canaanite legend, reinforced by the apocalypticism of Zoroastrian influences from the sixth century B.C.E. The violent metaphor of divine warfare and of a God who kills his son has become the central metaphor of the Master Story of Western culture. It has settled into the center of the psyche of the communities of faith we know as Judaism, Christianity, and Islam. Through them it has shaped the unconscious psychosocial assumptions of our cultures. This set of unconscious apocalyptic assumptions forms the sources and stage set for what we find meaningful in our cultures, from the violent game machines in the arcades our teenagers frequent to the actions of the Islamic Fundamentalist who flew airplanes into the World Trade Center. It is a short psychospiritual step from the vicarious forms of wishful mythic violence in the arcade machine to the mythic wishes that

---

Judaism, Christianity, and Islam, ed. J. Harold Ellens(Westport, CT: Praegar, 2001).

[127] Ibid., 3-5.

hurled gasoline-laded flying machines into the workplace of twenty thousand New Yorkers.

The hero-touting movies, popular literature, money-making music, and crowd-gathering Fundamentalist TV evangelists are all pushing the same apocalyptic model. Cosmic good and transcendental evil are depicted as being in mortal combat on the battlefields of our political policy, our international relations, our social values, and our spiritual questions.... Meanwhile, the truth is that none of this is so. But how many of the movies produced in the last 10 years would have gained any audience or financial success, if they had not exploited this false apocalyptic vision? What would happen to a movie that simply told the truth that humans are up against some massive challenges to form a congenial world, safe for children and those who love them? Who would make money on a film that refused the apocalyptic vision and instead set before us the hardheaded enigmas of the creation of a more blessed world?

...The Western world will need to decide whether it wishes to change this destructive story and its vicious core metaphors, or continue to wreak increasing psychospiritual havoc upon itself until the metaphor becomes so pervasive that we will all feel relieved with the impending prospect of a final cataclysmic Armageddon, closing out our history. Does this seem far-fetched? It is the palpable vision of the Zionist Christian Fundamentalists and Evangelicals, of the Islamic terrorists, and can it not be of the Israeli Zionist who would rather fight than switch? Such folk are serious and sincere about their vision and are quite sure they are closer to God's truth than any of the rest of us who seek spiritual authenticity and religious integrity and peace. The metaphor of cosmic evil and violence has taken over their center.[128]

I would only add two things to Ellen's contribution. One is that it is not just religion that has absorbed this ancient, false, ideology. From Freemasonry through Marxism, this seed is present in all our cultural, philosophical, and even scientific representations of reality. The other thing I would add is that this archetype, this "master story", did not just appear magically out of thin air. It was seeded and inserted into the human consciousness by the activities of the elite who exploit this mythology in order to invoke violence and control human populations. If you are a rich colonizing politician and you want to incite your population to colonial violence, all you have to do is invoke this archetype and you are good to go. This archetype, this master story, is a necessary precursor to violence and control. If we didn't have this archetype, if we didn't believe in good and evil, if we didn't buy into the Stars Wars propaganda, and if we believed the truth, which is that bad behavior and violence arises from ideological indoctrination into ancient old energy archetypes, toxic experiences, poverty, and violence in our own childhoods, we would be much less likely to pick up arms and go hurt other people. It just doesn't make any sense to beat and kill people who are themselves simply victims of violence and abuse.

In the next section on the Western tarot deck we will take a look at one example of how the elites of this planet, the so called .01 percent, seed and reproduce this old energy master story for their own special purposes. As a final case

---

[128] Ibid.

159

in point in this section, consider the psychopath. If there is any particular psychological disorder that represents our conception of "evil" in the world, it is the psychopath. Psychopaths, who are now diagnosed not as psychopaths but as individuals with antisocial personality disorders *(ASPD)*, are self-centred, manipulative, amoral, socially maladjusted, impulsive, aggressive, and sometimes violent. Those with ASPD have no conscience and don't care how much they hurt others. No doubt Hitler had ASPD, as do many of our other world leaders, corporate executives, media pundits, actors, and others who are involved in indoctrinating the population.[129] But note, people develop ASPD as a result of toxic environments and toxic socialization and not because they have "given in" to the dark side. As Martens points out, many researchers have made the link between ASPD and toxic environments.

> ...chronic antisocial behavior in children is the direct outcome of a breakdown in parental family management. Patterson constructed a model of the dual variables that sketches the process that leads to the development of antisocial children. The parents of antisocial children often come from disadvantaged families characterized by increased mobility, financial difficulties, negative changes in social attitudes, divorce, sexual abuse, and working women. These children are mostly raised by antisocial and/or single parents, frequently divorced women or those in transition, or unmarried adolescents. These parents are frequently unskilled and live isolated in a disorganized neighbourhood. As a result of an interaction between these factors and other variables

---

[129] Ronson, *The Psychopath Test: A Journey through the Madness Industry.*

(i.e., lack of parental care, poor diet, and parental substance abuse), their infants and toddlers become difficult to handle and at an older age show antisocial behavior. This model... is well supported by research.[130]

In other words, psychopaths are not "born this way," they are created in the violent crucibles of their toxic childhood experiences.

THE OLD ENERGY TAROT

Star Wars with its "good versus evil" archetype is an example of a vehicle for the wide dissemination of old energy archetypes, but it is hardly the only example. In our day and age, Hollywood, teachers, the mass media, and other what I would call **Agents of Consciousness**[181] join in and unconsciously (and sometimes consciously) participate in sowing and nurturing old energy archetypes, and resisting and destroying any new energy seeds that may appear. The thing with George Lucas is that he may not have been doing it on purpose. Like artists often do, he may have just been unconsciously (or uncritically) tapping into archetypes already there, or that he learned as a child. In other words, he may have been unintentionally reflecting old energy archetypes. Many people do this.

Willem H. J. Martens, "Antisocial and Psychopathic Personality Disorders: Causes, Course, and Remission—a Review Article," *International Journal of Offender Therapy and Comparative Criminology* 44, no. 4 (2000). Rutter, M, and M. Rutter. 1993. *Developing Minds: Challenge and Continuity Across the Life Span.* New York: Basic Books.

[131] http://spiritwiki.lightningpath.org/Agents_of_Consciousness

Many people unconsciously and uncritically ape old energy archetypes without ever realizing they are doing it. How many of the zealots who go to a Star Wars movie ever question the Christian/Judaic roots of their religious fever? The answer is, probably none. They accept the ideology, incorporate it into their center, and believe themselves superior from their fundamentalist spiritual counterparts, even though they are exactly the same. They reproduce the archetypes in their daily thinking, but they do it with the unconscious innocence of the unaware child.

Unfortunately, not everybody is a mere archetypal dupe of the System. As surprising as it may sound to some, people often actively work to create, re-create, and maintain old energy archetypes. Nowhere is this clearer than in the case of the "modern" Western Tarot deck. The modern western tarot deck is the classic case of the Family manipulating the mass consciousness of the planet by seeding and reinforcing old energy archetypes. I wrote an article about this entitled *The Sociology of Tarot.*[132] In that article I trace the development of an entire collection of old energy archetypes to the elite machinations of Freemasons during the transition from Feudalism to Capitalism. There I show how members of the Family (i.e. the new emerging capitalist class and the "old money" royal elites) worked together in their secret and exclusive "lodges" to develop and disseminate into the collective consciousness of this planet old energy religious/spiritual archetypes supportive of the new capitalist regime of

---

[132] Sosteric, "A Sociology of Tarot." Find it at
http://ejournals.library.ualberta.ca/index.php/CJS/article/view/2
0000

accumulation they were developing. Family members coopted the common *tarot deck,* imposed their own elite ideas onto the images of the deck, and then used that deck to disseminate their old energy archetypes to the people of the planet.

Their work began with the publication of a book by three famous nobles and Freemasons entitled *Le Monde Primitif* ("The Primeval World"). In that book are two essays which purport to reveal the "ancient esoteric history" of the tarot deck. The authors talk about the tarot's roots in ancient Egypt, in esoteric secret knowledge, and in the wisdom of Godlike characters who come to Earth to bring divine wisdom to the "worthy." These two essays purport to establish the divine/esoteric authority of the tarot, but in fact, the essays are nothing more than elaborate fabrications. To be blunt, the authors lie about the tarot deck and its origins. Why? They do this in order to create an aura of esoteric and spiritual mystery and authority. The mystery and the authority elevated the perceived importance of the deck and made people searching for the truth more psychologically open to the old energy lies inside, and it worked. Their lies were subsequently picked up by other elite authors in a centuries long effort to create the perfect vehicle for old energy indoctrination. As I state in my article on the sociology of tarot:

> Work had to be done on this game to establish its 'occult authority'. Elite authors (many of them high-level Freemasons) throughout the eighteenth, nineteenth and twentieth centuries established the authority of the tarot in a curiously anti-intellectual fashion, citing not the actual history of the deck (which could never have supported their claims to its

occult authority) but instead pointing to a fabricated history of legend based on fanciful and metaphysical imagination. They also exploited incestuous citation practices (citing one another's works as authorities), and also relied heavily on what Dummett (1980, 124) calls 'false ascription.' False ascription is a rhetorical strategy designed to bolster authority of a phenomenon by attributing it, or commentary on it, to some form of authoritative source. In the case of the tarot, the authoritative source could be an ancient philosopher, a mythological figure, an esoteric tradition, or whatever else could be conceived of. Over and over, we find authors of tarot books and cards making outrageous claims about the deck, developing false lineages, attributing it to mythological forces, making ridiculous epistemological and ontological claims, and generally going to great lengths to ignore history and establish the authority of the tarot.[133]

The centuries long effort culminated in the work of Arthur Edward Waite. A.E. Waite was a high level freemason who basically penned the modern tarot bible.[134] He brought together all the previous work of his "brothers," created the quintessential masonic tarot deck in 1910, which was titled the *Rider-Waite* tarot deck, and then sat back and watched as his deck become the stamp from which all other modern decks are taken,[135] with nobody being any the wiser.

---

[133] Ibid.

[134] Arthur Edward Waite, *The Pictorial Key to the Tarot: Being Fragments of a Secret Tradition under the Veil of Divination*(London: Rider, 1911).

[135] It is true that over the past couple of decades many people have attempted to draw "alternative" decks. Nowadays there are pixie

The masons were incredibly successful in seeding old energy archetypes and disseminating these into the mass consciousness of this planet. They were so successful that Decker, Depaulis, and Dummet call the tarot the

> **...most successful propaganda campaign ever launched**: not by a very long way the most important, but the most completely successful. An entire false history, and false interpretation, of the Tarot pack was concocted by the occultists; and it is all but universally believed".[136]

At this point it should be clear that people (and by "people" I mean members of the Family) intentionally get together to manipulate mass consciousness. To be sure, a lot of the old energy indoctrination, while clearly representative of ancient archetypes, emerges out of unconscious, innocent work. People like George Lucas, Stephen King, and other artists and musicians who work to recreate and distribute old energy archetypes probably do so without knowing exactly what they are doing; but, this is

---

decks and dark decks and sci-fi decks and a wealth of decks; but for all the alternative effort and artistic variation, they all bear the masonic imprint of the A.E. Wait deck. Masonic decks are easy to identify. If a tarot deck has a fool card, then it is a deck that is derived from the masonic stamp. See Michael Sharp, *The Book of the Triumph of Spirit: Old and New Energy Archetypes*, Triumph of Spirit (St. Albert: Lightning Path Press, 2017).

[136] Ronald Decker, Thierry Depaulis, and Michael Dummett, *A Wicked Pack of Cards: The Origins of the Occult Tarot*(New York: St Martin's Press, 1996), 27.emphasis added. See also Michael Dummett, *The Game of Tarot*(London: Duckwork, 1980); Ronald Decker and Michael Dummett, *A History of the Occult Tarot, 1870-1970*(London: Duckworth, 2002).

not always the case. As we have seen with the tarot deck, elite members of the Family do get together to intentionally construct ideology and intentionally manipulate consciousness.

This is an important point. Family members are not stupid. As the case of the tarot deck illustrates, they have worked for centuries on developing old energy archetypes that provide the basis for ongoing global exploitation. If we want to change the world, we (and by "we" I mean those interested in saving the planet) have to do the same sort of archetypal work. We have to construct archetypes and disseminate ideas that do not bring forward ancient Mesopotamian ideology and that do not provide ideological support for exploitation and accumulation.

I won't kid you about this, that is going to be tough. Sorting out all the old energy ideas that the Family has used to support their regimes of accumulation, removing them from the mass consciousness of this planet, and replacing them with salutatory and emancipating new energy ideas, is going to be a challenge for a couple of reasons at least. On the one hand there is the challenge of coming up with new energy ideas. If you think back to the centuries long effort of Freemasons to establish their Family tarot deck, you can see this is a complicated and time-consuming process. Even if you could just sit down and channel a bunch of new energy archetypes into the world, they would still need development, publication, distribution, and uptake by artists and others who work with these archetypes. That's a lot of work. And given the Family's obvious resistance to facilitating the process, a major challenge lies ahead.

Another challenge with removing old energy archetypes and replacing them with new ones is that old energy archetypes are deeply embedded and ubiquitous, and it is very easy to reproduce them even when you are trying hard not to. For example, there are many progressives who would totally deny any allegiance to the old energy archetypes of the Catholic Church but who nevertheless attend a Star Wars movie with the same reverence the faithful attend a religious service. They buy into the duality between good and evil in the same uncritical fashion that the faithful do every day. Convincing these faithful of the need to stop reproducing the archetypes, and convincing them of the need to change their thinking to ensure they don't unwittingly continue to reproduce the old energy archetypes, would be just as difficult as changing the minds of the Christian or Buddhist faithful. And of course, it not just the Christians and the Lucasifarians who may resist. As noted, Marxists have brought the old energy archetypes unwittingly forward as well. Their use of the old energy archetypes is deeply embedded in their prideful presentation of the philosophical/dialectical of history and I can anticipate strong resistance as well.

So what's the step forward here? Well, regardless of any resistance we might face, the next step forward is to actually do the work of identifying old energy archetypes and replacing them with new. I myself have done a bit of work in this direction. For example, I have written a new energy genesis story entitled *The Song of Creation: The Story of Genesis*.[137] This story, which needs to be animated, voiced,

---

[137] Michael Sharp, *The Song of Creation: The Story of Genesis* (St. Albert: Lightning Path Press, 2006).

produced, and otherwise distributed, provides a spiritual story of creation that *does not* import any of the ancient Mesopotamian ideas of cosmic good and evil identified by Ellens earlier.[138] That story, which is written as an epic poem, is complex, but in essence it removes the "basis of exploitation" (which as we have seen is justification of violence) and provides an alternative archetypal foundation (a new energy story) aimed at fostering planetary unity and unified cosmic purpose. In that story the cosmic forces of good do not duke it out with the cosmic forces of evil. In that story there is no violent checkboard of black and white, and there is absolutely no justification for violence at all. In that story we (and by "we") I mean all souls, participate as equal members in a "cosmic plan" aimed at creating a glorious playground for spirit. It is an archetypal story of unity and oneness that is as far removed from the ancient Mesopotamian myths of duality as human beings are from the one celled organic soup from which our physical body's emerged.

The Song of Creation is not my only contribution to developing new energy archetypes to replace the old energy archetypes of accumulation and exploitation. I have also been working on an alternative tarot deck and a set of book resources that a) unpacks the Family's old energy archetypes and b) provides a complete set of new energy archetypes that can be used to form the basis for artistic, political, economic, and even philosophical expression. If you are interested, I discuss the Family's use of tarot as well as key archetypes, archetypal revision, deprogramming the System, and a set of new energy archetypes in greater detail

---

[138] Ellens, "Introduction: The Destructive Power of Religion."

in my *Book of the Triumph of Spirit* series.[139] In that book series, which has a strong spiritual focus, I provide *new* archetypes in a new tarot deck, which I call the Triumph of Spirit deck, that do not reflect the masonic stamp. A short summary of the basic ideas, a summary of the progress of the project, and a list of available resources, and an indication of the progress of the project, are available on the Triumph of Spirit website.[140]

DAMAGE TO THE PHYSICAL UNIT

By now it should be clear that if we are to change our values and change the world we have to a) transform hostile environments, b) clean up corrupted ideologies, and c) develop and replace *old energy* archetypes with *new energy* archetypes. A **fourth challenge/obstacle** to changing values and transforming the world is healing the hatred, anger, resentment, and damage to the body (the physical unit) that arises as a result of the violent and toxic socialization we all experience as we grow up within the System. And we do experience damage. A wealth of recent and rapidly expanding research has demonstrated that the violent (spanking, getting screamed at), abusive, and neglectful experiences of our childhood damages our

---

[139] Sharp, *The Book of the Triumph of Spirit: Old and New Energy Archetypes*; *The Book of the Triumph of Spirit: Healing and Activating with the Halo/Sharp System*(St. Albert: Lightning Path Press, 2013); *The Book of the Triumph of Spirit: Master's Key*(St Albert, Alberta: Lightning Path Press, Unpublished).

[140] See http://triumphofspirit.lightningpath.org/

physical body and mind in profound ways.[141] Violence and abuse, whether in childhood, adolescence, or adulthood, leads to a host of negative emotional, psychological, and physical sequela including depression, substance dependence and abuse, eating disorders, personality disorders, post-traumatic stress disorders, suicidal ideation, lower grade performance, dysfunctional personal relationships, and even increased incidence of physical disease. Researchers have demonstrated that even something as seemingly benign as psychological and emotional neglect (i.e. failing to snuggle, cuddle, love, and kiss young infants and children) can lead to a profound breakdown in our human ability to empathize and connect, a breakdown that is rooted in damage to the physical brain. Indeed, one study found that neurobiological mechanisms of emotion, empathy, attachment, and social functioning were seriously damaged by simple lack of physical contact (read emotional, psychological, and physical neglect) in early infanthood.[142]

Damage to our ability to empathize and connect is a serious concern for us here. The solution to the global crisis caused by the Family's regime of accumulation requires us all to make empathic connections to humans

---

[141] For a summary of the research see the SpiritWiki page at http://spiritwiki.lightningpath.org/Toxic_Socialization.

[142] Alison B. Wismer Fries et al., "Early Experience in Humans Is Associated with Changes in Neuropeptides Critical for Regulating Social Behavior," *Proceedings of the National Academy of Sciences of the United States of America* 102, no. 47 (2005).

of all stripes, and even to the dying planet itself. These empathic connections are what will help motivate, ground, and make permanent the required value change, and it is the value change that will help us reject the Family's regime and move us to replace it with something new. But if we don't really care about what is happening to other people, if we cannot make empathic connections to the planet, animals, humans, and our fellow humans, then unless we actually experience the environmental, economic, or political fallout of the Family's activities (i.e. if it is not us losing our homes, families, and lives in tornadoes, war, and poverty) for ourselves, we won't be bothered to even think about it, much less make any of the required changes.

And of course, it not just the fact that toxic socialization has (perhaps deliberately) undermined our ability to connect and empathize with others. When we are damaged in our childhood we have difficulty acting in **aligned** ways. Indeed, and as we have seen with research on psychopathic violence, bitter, angry, hurt, and damaged people often *act out* in violent ways. The least damaged act out violently towards family members (because family members are usually the safest), while the most damaged act out with strangers, and/or in criminal ways. Even if damaged individuals can manage positive views and positive actions, often it is superficial window dressing over a damaged inside core. And if it is superficial window dressing over a damaged core, then any outward attestation of higher values is often a hypocritical cover over the hurt, angry, and damaged being that is inside.

I have told this story before about an old neighbor of ours who dressed herself and her home up in all the positive spiritual accoutrements she could find, yet was bitter and angry deep inside. Tibetan singing bowls, angels in the doorway, incense in the burning bowl, and the latest "wisdom words" from the latest new age guru were out on display. Superficially she was all about love, acceptance, egalitarianism, equality, and all the higher spiritual virtues. In reality, she was filled with anger and hatred. Her "darkness" expressed itself violently in her interactions with those less powerful than her, i.e. her children, which she neglected and abused when she thought no one was looking.

Do not get me wrong, I'm not pointing fingers. I am just identifying a particular reality we all live with. Her situation is just a snapshot of the mental, emotional, and spiritual pathology that exists all around us, but that is obscured by the reality obscuring hypocrisy that many of us engage in. Abuse of one's less powerful children is the same as abuse and exploitation of spouses, employees, and even entire nations. It is rooted in the same ideology that justifies abuse, the same archetypes which excuse exploitation, and the same toxic pathology. And once again let me say, I am not here to judge anybody. I am certainly no angel when it comes to dealing with children. The damage I have done to my oldest child as the result of my selfish immaturity is so bad that he won't even talk to me. We do what we can to fix it, and then we move on. I'm just saying, bitter, angry, hurt, and damaged people have a hard time making authentic empathic connections, have difficulty thinking and acting in aligned ways, and struggle with authentic, non-hypocritical, value change, despite their proclamations to hold lofty spiritual, humanistic, scientific, or religious values. And arguably, the problem has gotten worse in this late stage of the Family's now globalized accumulation regime. The level of pain and suffering caused by the Regime is horrendous,[143] and more damage is created every day. So where does this leave our efforts to "stick" authentic value change? If we, as a global community, are going to stick authentic value change, our toxic socialization practices will have to cease immediately so that we stop turning out children without the ability to empathize and connect with others. Not only that, but the damage, hurt, and pain most of us have experienced, and that disconnects us and makes global unity difficult, will need to be addressed. In other words, we will all need to heal.

Actually buckling down and healing the planet is going to take a lot of work. The damage is severe and therapy, even with sophisticated methods, can take a long time. Healing is not a question of simply releasing negativity or rubbing singing bowls. The emotional and psychological mess that many of us deal with requires serious attention and work. If that isn't enough of a challenge, there is a serious shortage of qualified healers, and the healing professions are only now beginning to understand just how deep the

---

[143] I'm taking as evidence here out of control gun violence in the U.S. the ridiculously high rate of anti-depressant usage in North America, and the deadly toll of rising suicide rates, at least in the U.S.A. If you are not in the U.S.A, Pratt LA, Brody DJ, and Gu Q, "Antidepressant Use in Persons Aged 12 and Over: United States, 2005-2008. Nchs Data Brief, No 76.," ed. National Center for Health Statistics, NCHS Data Brief (Hyattsville, MD2011); Center for Disease Control, "Suicide among Adults Aged 35-64 Years — United States, 1999-2010," *Morbidity and Mortality Weekly Report (MMWR)* 62, no. 17 (2013).

damage may be.[144] The only way to address and heal the damage is to provide more avenues for authentic healing and authentic therapeutic practice. This is important. *If we want to transform the world, we have to stop hurting our children and we need to start healing the people.* If we want to heal the people, we need more competent healers, more therapists, more mentors, more life coaches, and a shift in priorities away from greedy materialism and selfish accumulation and towards more aligned priorities and values. These are all necessary precursors to global transformation.

The path ahead of us is surely a challenging one, but it is not impossible. The biggest challenge is making a sufficient enough shift early on so that we can devote the necessary resources for the long-term task ahead. The problem is, we have to make the shift fast. The globe is currently teetering on the brink of financial and economic disaster caused by the Family's accumulation regime. This disaster is going to be exacerbated by technology like self-driving cars which threaten to decimate entire industries.[145] The problem, other than the obvious consequences of this disruption, is that it is going to happen fast making it impossible (under the current economic regime) for labor markets to adjust

---

[144] For a summary of what we currently know, see http://spiritwiki.lightningpath.org/Toxic_Socialization.

[145] Scott Santens, "Self-Driving Trucks Are Going to Hit Us Like a Human-Driven Truck," *Medium.com*, May 14 2015; Adam Hayes, "The Unintended Consequences of Self-Driving Cars " *Investopedia*, September 2 2015; Chunka Mui, "Will Driverless Cars Force a Choice between Lives and Jobs?," *Forbes*, December 19 2013.

fast enough. Self-driving cars will surely have replaced human labor by 2025, and car ownership will likely be plummeting off a cliff by then as well.[146] Unless we begin planning for this and other forms of technological disruption on the way immediately, the humanitarian crises going on now is going to look like a Sunday walk through the park. Unfortunately, the only way we are going to be able to start planning is if a substantial majority of people suddenly wake up to the problem, shift their values, and suddenly begin making revolutionary changes in the economic, political, and social regimes of this planet. If that doesn't happen quickly, there's no hope on the horizon for millions, maybe billions, of people on this planet.

AUTHENTIC MYSTICAL CONNECTION

I have made it clear that if we are to save ourselves and this planet we need a fundamental shift in values. We have also seen that lack of alternatives, corrupted old energy archetypes, buried trauma covered over with hypocritical expressions of higher values, damage in our childhoods, and ongoing suffering and hurt make the practical realization of authentic value change difficult, but it is not impossible. There is a way to materialize almost instant value change and that is through the practice of a sophisticated and **authentic spirituality**[147] aimed at teaching

---

[146] Beth Braverman, "This Is a Big Problem for the Auto Industry – and It's Getting Worse " *The Fiscal Times*, January 19 2016.

[147] For more details, see the SpiritwWiki page at http://spiritwiki.lightningpath.org/Authentic_Spirituality.

people to have significant and deep **mystical connection**.[148] In my view, without authentic spirituality leading to deep mystical connection, there is no foundation upon which to build authentic value change. Without deep mystical connection, the sort of rapid value change that is required is simply impossible.

Of course, after reading the above many readers may have spit their coffee all over the page. Surely I am either joking, or crazy. Spirituality and religion cannot be the path forward. Despite having had thousands of years to move the planet forward, and despite eschatological promise to achieve the same,[149] neither New Thought, fundamental spirituality, nor any point in between has been able to achieve the sort of mass transformation of values that is required. Nevertheless, I am serious. The key to planetary transformation, the missing piece to our global salvation, is authentic spirituality and authentic mystical experience.

At this point let us ask the obvious question: what is authentic spirituality? That's simple. As I explain in *Rocket Scientists' Guide to Authentic Spirituality*,[150] authentic spirituality is spirituality that works. More specifically,

---

[148] Mystical connection, or just "connection" for short, is the LP term for what occurs when your body's mind connects with some "higher" level of consciousness.

See http://spiritwiki.lightningpath.org/Connection for more details

[149] All traditional spiritualties make eschatological promises about end times doom and unfolding utopias.

[150] Michael Sharp, *The Rocket Scientists' Guide to Authentic Spirituality* (St. Albert, Alberta: Lightning Path Press, 2010).

authentic spirituality is spirituality that leads towards real and valid spiritual experience. Put in perhaps a more familiar way, authentic spiritualties are those that lead to authentic mystical experience.

Authentic spirituality => mystical experience

To use nomenclature I have developed, *authentic spiritualties are spiritualties that lead to authentic connection to the* **Fabric of Consciousness**.[151]

And just why is authentic mystical connection to the *Fabric of Consciousness* so important? In my view, and in the context of the growing ecological, psychological, economic, and political crises of this world, connection to the Fabric facilitated by the wise guidance of an authentic spirituality *is the foundation for global value change and global*

------

[151] I coined the term *Fabric of Consciousness* back in 2006 in volume one of my Book of Light to describe what mystics from around the globe have called God, Brahman, Buddha Self, Wuji, Hunab Ku, Tao, Vishnu, Ain Soph, and so on. I coin the term primarily to move the discussion of God/Consciousness above the confusion that attends most understandings of God, and the baggage that attends most terminology. The term *Fabric of Consciousness* provides a clean conceptual slate upon which to build an understanding of the non-material realms of creation. The term is clean up front and does not participate in the sexist, classist, patriarchal, scientifically vacuous, and outdated confusion of traditional concepts.

If you are interested in learning more about the *Fabric of Consciousness*, I recommend my *Book of Light*. See *The Book of Light: The Nature of God, the Structure of Consciousness, and the Universe within You*, 4 vols., vol. one -air(St. Albert, Alberta: Lightning Path Press, 2006).

revolution.[152] Some may see this as a strong statement, but I will stand by it. Without authentic spiritualties leading to authentic mystical connection, there is no foundation for collective value change, no hope for global unity, and no fountain from which we may derive the spiritual sustenance necessary to stand and act (in alignment) to save the world. In other words, without an authentic spirituality there is, in my view, no hope.

---

[152] Discussing the nature and development of a modern authentic spirituality that could provide a path towards authentic mystical experience is beyond the scope of this work. Similarly, a discussion of authentic connection to The Fabric, what that is, how to facilitate it, and how to cope with it when it happens, is also out of bounds here. I have done a bit of thinking on the foundation and parameters of authentic spirituality and authentic spiritual practice, and am in the process of developing a "program" to facilitate said connection. For example, in *Rocket Scientists' Guide to Authentic Spirituality* I define authentic spirituality and discuss guidelines for distinguishing between authentic spirituality, i.e. those that lead to mystical experience, and those that lead towards disconnection. In *The Great Awakening: Concepts and Techniques for Successful Spiritual Practice* I provide basic advice on basic spiritual technique. I look in more depth at the origins and theory of it all in *Lightning Path Book One - Introduction to the Lightning Path*, ed. Michael Sharp, vol. 1, Lightning Path Lesson Series (St. Albert, Alberta: Lightning Path Press, 2014).

See *The Rocket Scientists' Guide to Authentic Spirituality; The Great Awakening: Concepts and Techniques for Successful Spiritual Practice*(St. Albert, Alberta, Canada: Lightning Path Press, 2007).

I imagine that a few readers may have some objection at this point, so let us pause for a moment and address these issues. **If you are traditionally religious**, you may balk at the notion that there is general lack of authentic spirituality, and you may resist any push to reevaluate your own spirituality to see whether it is an effective and authentic path. You may want to cling to the comfortable notion that your particular belief system provides you with authentic direction and guidance and if so, that is fine. I personally believe there is much legitimate spiritual wisdom in traditional world spirituality, though with everything else that is going on in them it may be difficult to sort out at times. I will remind you though, the world (and often even our own personal lives) is in a very bad state. Despite thousands of years of opportunity, traditional religions (and even modern New Age and New Thought varieties) have been unable to end the cycles of violence, greed, war, and destruction that regularly wash over the surface of this Earth. Indeed, New Age varieties seem only capable of helping damaged and disconnected people ignore the state of the world,[153] while traditional religion distracts us from

---

[153] The so-called "Law of Attraction" (LOA) is a New Age meme that was popularized a few years ago by a massive (and it should be noted quite expensive) global advertising campaign. According to this "teaching," if you pay attention or even think about bad things (like war, terrorism, debt, the sorry state of the global economy, etc.), you "attract" them to yourself. It is, so the pundits say, a universal cosmic law of creation! The (convenient for the Family) advice of LOA pundits to people frightened by the state of the world is to turn away. Don't pay attention to the war, violence, greed, and chaos because if you do you will attract it. Instead, turn away and pretend it is not there. By turning away and pretending it is not there, you will engage powerful universal

the real problem (which is the Family's accumulation Regime) by trying to convince us all that we are the problem because of our karma, sin, and bad behavior.[154] What's worse, traditional religions have often participated in the violence, greed, war, and destruction! Indeed, the

---

forces that will protect you from the darkness. In other words, if you don't look the reality won't be there. This basic violation of infant object permanence is stunning and absurd. It has nothing to do with any authentic spirituality and really only makes sense only as a propaganda campaign of delusion and distraction.

I would like to note here that the Law of Attraction is the quintessential expression of human disconnection and lack of empathy. The LOA actually teaches us to ignore and disconnect from human suffering and pain. In this regard the LOA may be popular and attractive spirituality to people because it reflects and provides a tacit excuse for all those individuals who have had their ability to connect, empathize, and relate *damaged* by toxic socialization experiences. In other words, the LOA is an ideology and excuse for toxic pathology, wrapped up in a sheep's skin of spiritual sophistication.

For additional commentary on the LOA see "Screwing the Population of the World: The Secret, the Law, and the Lie.," *The Sociology of Religion* 2016.

[154] It is true isn't it? Traditional spiritualties blame the state of the world on the "sins of people," while conveniently ignoring the economic regimes that are the root source of all the world's evils. According to traditional spiritualties, and even modern secular humanism, the world is the way it is because we are the problem. It is not the greedy imperialism fostered by our accumulation Regime that is the cause of our problem. The world is in the state it is in because we are violent, fallen, "ejected from the Garden," spiritual losers.

level of corruption displayed by the Catholic Church is positively infernal.[155] We may want to cling to our traditional belief systems, and indeed there may be something legitimate in traditional spirituality, especially when one goes directly to the words of the mystics and avatars who initiated the traditions,[156] but it may simply not

---

[155] An interesting overview of the violence, greed, war, and destruction that the Catholic Church, which is arguably one of the richest corporations in the world, is provided by Emily Stewart, "How Rich Is the Catholic Church?," *The Street*, September 22 2015. For a broad historical overview, see Gerald Posner, *God's Bankers: A History of Money and Power at the Vatican*(New York: Simon & Schuster, 2015). For an even more disturbing look at the activities of traditional religions, and how they support the Family, see Paul Williams, *Operation Gladio: The Unholy Alliance between the Vatican, the Cia, and the Mafia*(New York: Prometheus Books, 2015).

[156] As we will see below, all of the big religious institutions, be the Christian, Buddhist, Hindu, Mormon, etc., are all based on the words of individuals who have had mystical experiences. Jesus Christ, Mohammed, Joseph Smith, Buddha, and all others initiated religious traditions by speaking about their mystical connections. Reading the actual words of the mystics can often be very enlightening. The problem is, few of the faithful ever spend the time reading the actual words. Ironically, people who "follow" religions often do not follow the words of the individual mystics; they follow the words of the "interpreters" (i.e. priests, gurus, etc.) who interpose themselves between the "faithful" and the mystic (I know as a child I did). A typical Catholic service, for example, is all about a priest reading a passage from the bible and then explaining to the people what that passage really means. As a member of the faithful you may choose to trust the words of the interpreters put between you and the actual teachings of Jesus Christ, but after seeing the nefarious activities of wealthy

be enough to overcome the greed, corruption, and delusion and bring the changes necessary to save this planet. For this reason, it may be worthwhile expanding your horizon and taking a second look at the notion of authentic spirituality.

I imagine that religious folk are not the only ones that may balk at the notions of *authentic spirituality* and *mystical connection* being tabled here. **If you are critical of religion and spirituality**, if you are an atheist or agnostic, you may also balk at the notion that authentic spirituality is a precursor to value change or a foundation for global revolution. Your view of religion and spirituality may slide somewhere between the Freudian notion that religion is a distraction for the weak minded and the Marxian notion that it is a delusional opiate designed to manipulate the masses. I will not defend religion in this regard. It is true, as numerous scholars have pointed out, that religion can be delusion and that it has been a tool that the Family has used to distract, mollify, and confuse.[157] However it is also *true,* and you may scoff if you wish, that within religion there is an **authentic core**[158] of religious/mystical

_____

institutions like the Catholic Church (see footnote 155), a critical second look may be in order.

[157] Sigmund Freud, *The Future of an Illusion*(New York: Anchor Books, 1964). Karl Marx, *A Contribution to the Critique of Hegel's Philosophy of Right*(Cambridge: Cambridge University Press, 1970); Peter Berger, *The Sacred Canopy: Elements of a Sociological Theory of Religion*(New York: Anchor Books, 1969).

[158] The authentic core of relgion is mystical/religious experience. See http://spiritwiki.lightningpath.org/Authentic_Core

experience. This authentic core provides for powerful and transformative personal and collective transformation and change. It might sound strange to some, but I am not the first scholar to suggest this. Over the decades several scholars have taken serious interest in the "authentic core" of human religious experience. William James, esteemed father of American Psychology, suggested mystical experience was the transformative bedrock of religion.[159] Wayne Proudfoot called religious experience ubiquitous and stated that "Religion has always been an experiential matter. It is not just a set of creedal statements or a collection of rites."[160] Heriot-Maitland noted that "the origin of a given tradition can often be traced to an initial transcendent encounter, moment of revelation,"[161] (or what I would call a connection to The Fabric). Abraham Maslow, a psychologist who spent the bulk of his career looking at "peak experiences" writes:

> The very beginning, the intrinsic core, the essence, the universal nucleus of every known high religion... has been the private, lonely, personal illumination, revelation, or ecstasy of some acutely sensitive prophet or seer. The high religions call themselves revealed religions and *each of them tends to rest its validity, its function, and its right to exist on the codification and the communication of this original*

[159] William James, *The Varieties of Religious Experience: A Study of Human Nature* (New York: Penguin, 1982), 6.

[160] Wayne Proudfoot, *Religious Experience* (California: University of California Press, 1985), xi.

[161] Charles P. Heriot-Maitland, "Mysticism and Madness: Different Aspects of the Same Human Experience?," *Mental Health, Religion & Culture* 11, no. 3 (2008): 302.

mystic experience or revelation from the lonely prophet to the mass of human beings in general.[162]

William Stace echoes Maslow when he points out that Vedantism, a leading philosophy of India, is an intellectualization of a "reality rooted in mysticism."[163] Indeed Stace, who is one of the biggest contributors to the study of mystical experience in modern times, called mystical experience "a psychological fact of which there is abundant evidence." He further went on to say that "To deny or doubt that it exists as a psychological fact is not a reputable opinion. It is ignorance and very stupid."[164]

Stace grounds his strong statement, no doubt, on the historical ubiquity of mystical experience. The truth is, mystical/religious experience has been a feature of our existence for millennia.[165] From the earliest emergence of humanity in the primeval muck[166] to our current modern experiences, mystical experience is a fact. The reality is that anywhere between 20.5 percent and 53 percent of Americans have had mystical/ religious experiences as

[162] A. H. Maslow, "The "Core-Religious" or "Transcendent" Experience," in *The Highest State of Consciousness*, ed. John White(New York: Doubleday, 2012), 339.emphasis added

[163] Walter Terence Stace, *The Teachings of the Mystics*(New York: Mentor, 1960), 30.

[164] Ibid., 14.

[165] Dean H Hamer, *The God Gene: How Faith Is Hardwired into Our Genes*(New York: Anchor, 2005).

[166] Ibid.; Andew Newberg, Eugene d'Aquile, and Vince Rause, *Why God Won't Go Away: Brain Science and the Biology of Belief*, ed. New York(New York: Ballantine Books, 2001).

such,[167] many with total spontaneity (i.e. without even trying!). And note, it is not just the uneducated or the religious who have these experiences. Contrary to what dogmatists like Richard Dawkins would have you believe,[168] the limited sociological research that has been conducted on the phenomenon has found that those with more education are equally likely, if not more likely, to have profound mystical experiences.[169] The educated just do not always conceptualize it in the same way. Instead of using religious language and concepts, they use a secular language, a psychologically neutral language (characterizing mystical connection as a peak experience for example)[170] and they step back from the personalized patriarch of mass

---

[167] David Yamane and Megan Polzer, "Ways of Seeing Ecstasy in Modern Society: Experiential-Expressive and Cultural-Linguistic Views," *Sociology of Religion* 55, no. 1 (1994); Rodney Stark, *What Americans Really Believe*(Waco, Texas: Baylor University Press, 2008); Linda Brookover Bourque, "Social Correlates of Transcendental Experiences," *Sociological Analysis* 30, no. 3 (1969); Linda Brookover Bourque and Kurt W. Back, "Language, Society and Subjective Experience," *Sociometry* 34, no. 1 (1971)..

[168] Richard Dawkins, *The God Delusion*(New York: Mariner Books, 2006).

[169] Bourque, "Social Correlates of Transcendental Experiences."; Bourque and Back, "Language, Society and Subjective Experience."

[170] Maslow, "A Theory of Human Motivation."; A. H. Maslow, *Motivation and Personality (2nd Ed.)*(New York: Harper & Row, 1970); *Religions, Values, and Peak Experiences*(Columbus: Ohio State University Press, 1964).),

religion[171] and instead prefer to discuss self-actualization, transcendence,[172] "pure consciousness events,"[173] or as Albert Einstein put it, *cosmic religious feeling.*[174]

I want to pause for a moment and consider in a bit more detail the views of Albert Einstein. Einstein is often invoked by atheists and deists alike to support either a simplistic atheism or a simplistic deism; but his views were more complex and nuanced. As you might expect, Einstein clearly and unequivocally rejected the personalized patriarch, the "God conceived in man's image," as presented by the priests of mass religion;[175] nevertheless he did feel a mystical reverence for life and a connection to a transcendent God as expressed through nature and felt in religious experience. It was God, but not a God as most would understand. For Einstein there was something of

---

[171] Elaine Howard Ecklund, *What Scientists Really Think*(Oxford: Oxford University Press, 2012); Elaine Howard Ecklund and Elizabeth Long, "Scientists and Spirituality," *Sociology of Religion* 72, no. 3 (2011).

[172] Maslow, *The Farther Reaches of Human Nature.*

[173] Robert K.S. Forman, *Mysticism, Mind, Consciousness*(Albany: State University of New York, 1999).

[174] Einstein speaks directly and clearly about *religious experience* in his 1930 New York Times article entitled *Religion and Science. Albert Einstein, "Religion and Science," New York Times, November 9 1930.*

The full text of Einstein's article is available http://www.sacred-texts.com/aor/einstein/einsci.htm.

[175] Gary E. Bowman, "Einstein and Mysticism," *Zygon: Journal of Religion & Science* 49, no. 2 (2014).

great intelligence, a "marvellous order" that was manifest in nature *and* human thought. Einstein approached this marvellous order with a feeling of reverence or, in his own words, cosmic religious feeling. Einstein saw religious geniuses, i.e. prophets and Avatars of old, as expressing and developing this cosmic religious feeling. Some readers may find this doubtful, so it is worth quoting at length from his 1930 article.

> The individual feels the futility of human desires and aims and the sublimity and marvelous order which reveal themselves both in nature and in the world of thought.... The beginnings of cosmic religious feeling already appear at an early stage of development, e.g., in many of the Psalms of David and in some of the Prophets. Buddhism, as we have learned especially from the wonderful writings of Schopenhauer, contains a much stronger element of this.

> The religious geniuses of all ages have been distinguished by this kind of religious feeling, which knows no dogma and no God conceived in man's image; so that there can be no church whose central teachings are based on it. Hence it is precisely among the heretics of every age that we find men who were filled with this highest kind of religious feeling and were in many cases regarded by their contemporaries as atheists, sometimes also as saints. Looked at in this light, men like Democritus, Francis of Assisi, and Spinoza are closely akin to one another. [176]

In conversations with Dr. Hermanns, a sociologist and poet, Einstein revealed his conceptions of God and mysticism. Einstein says that he "no longer believed in the

---

[176] Einstein, "Religion and Science."

known God of the Bible, but rather in the mysterious God expressed in nature,"[177] a God which he felt revealed "such an intelligence that any human logic falters in comparison."[178] He even admitted to mystical connection when he said to Hermanns, "We both may have mystical connections, but my God appears as the physical world."[179] Einstein found his mystical connection with the natural world, which is something that any mystic would also feel a connection to. Indeed, Einstein describes his mystical experiences and cosmic religious feelings in exactly the same way a mystic would, which is to say, as unity, oneness, and wholeness. Hermanns writes:

> Einstein looked through the window and seemed to mumble more to the trees than to me, "I believe that I have cosmic religious feelings. I never could grasp how one could satisfy these feelings by praying to limited objects. The tree outside is life, a statue is dead. The whole of nature is life, and life, as I observe it, rejects a God resembling man. I like to experience the universe as one harmonious whole. Every cell has life.[180]

Finally, it should be noted that Einstein was not the only famous physicist to speak in mystical terms. Ken Wilbur put together a collection of the "mystical writings" of the world's great physicists in which he claims that every

---

[177] William Hermanns, *Einstein and the Poet* (Boston: Branden Books, 1983), 9.

[178] Ibid., 83.

[179] Ibid., 71.

[180] Ibid., 63.

physicist in his volume was an actual, dyed-in-the-wool, mystic.[181]

I am hopeful that at this point your interest in mystical/religious/cosmic experience has been tweaked. A careful look at the historical record reveals that many scientists, even the very smartest ones, have thought seriously about the issue. Indeed, when we open the field, harmonize our definitions, consider that there is a secular language of mystical experience that even Einstein used, and look at the facts, it seems that mystical experience is far more common that even the high water mark of 54% suggests. Indeed, when we tear down the tower of babel we find that mystical experience is a common, ubiquitous, even normal experience for human beings. Abraham Maslow was perhaps the first to note this remarkable fact at the same time that he suggested that those who did not (or could not) have mystical experiences were dealing with some form of psychological fear or pathology:

> In my first investigations... I thought some people had peak-experiences and others did not. But as I gathered information, and as I became more skilful in asking questions, I found that a higher and higher percentage of my subjects began to report peak-experiences.... I finally fell into the habit of expecting everyone to have peak-experiences and of being rather surprised if I ran across somebody who could report none at all. Because of this experience, *I finally began to use the word "non-peaker" to describe, not the person who is unable to have peak-experiences, but rather the person who is afraid of them, who*

---

[181] Ken Wilber, *Quantum Questions: Mystical Writings of the World's Great Physicists* (New York: Shambhala, 2001).

*suppresses them, who denies them, who turns away
from them, or who "forgets" them.* [182]

The notion that mystical experience in particular, and
spirituality more generally, remains significant and
ubiquitous is backed by recent research. Despite the fact
that church attendance has dropped off over the years,
atheism has not expanded significantly. Only about 3% of
American's identify themselves as committed atheists, and
the numbers aren't that impressive anywhere else. We
have nine percent in Canada, twelve percent in Norway
and Germany, and a "staggering" nineteen percent in
France. [183] Clearly, the world is not beating a pathway to the
"higher rationality" of the atheist perspective. And
speaking of the "higher rationality" of atheism, there is
sometimes very little in the way of reason and rationality in
the thoughts and opinions of the atheist. As Einstein noted,
and as the dogmatist Richard Dawkins has amply
demonstrated, atheists can be just as fanatical and dogmatic
as any fundamentalist religious fanatic. Einstein had some
particularly harsh words for the fanatical atheists of this
world.

> I was barked at by numerous dogs who are earning
> their food guarding ignorance and superstition for the
> benefit of those who profit from it. Then there are
> the fanatical atheists whose intolerance is of the same
> kind as the intolerance of the religious fanatics and

---

[182] Maslow, "The "Core-Religious" or "Transcendent" Experience,"
340-1.emphasis added

[183] Bruce Hunsberger and Bob Altemeyer, *Atheists: A
Groundbreaking Study of America's Nonbelievers*(New York:
Prometheus Books, 2006).

comes from the same source. They are like slaves who are still feeling the weight of their chains which they have thrown off after hard struggle. They are creatures who—in their grudge against the traditional "opium of the people"—cannot bear the music of the spheres. The Wonder of nature does not become smaller because one cannot measure it by the standards of human moral and human aims.[184]

And lest one still wishes to discount mystical experience, peak experiences, or cosmic religious feeling as stupid irrationality, be aware that the last ten years of neuro-scientific research has demonstrated the validity of mystical experiences, and their general salutatory effect on mental and emotional health.[185] Whatever mystical, religious, occult experience happens to be, whether it is connection to actual higher consciousness or a mere neurological artefact of human evolution, it is significant and worthy of concerted scholarly and layperson attention.

So what does this all have to do with value change, accumulation, money, and saving the planet? As I argue above, *mystical experience* provides the foundation, or at least part of the foundation, for authentic, rigorous and permanent value change, a change that I would argue we need to achieve on a global scale, and fast. It is not as outrageous as the critics might claim. Over the centuries

---

[184] Einstein quoted in Max Jammer, *Einstein and Religion*(New Jersey: Princeton University Press, 1999), 97.

[185] Andrew Newberg and Mark Robert Waldman, *How God Changes Your Brain: Breakthrough Findings from a Leading Neuroscientist*(New York: Ballantine Books, 2009); Newberg, d'Aquile, and Rause, *Why God Won't Go Away: Brain Science and the Biology of Belief.*

many people have experienced positive, progressive, significant, and instant value change as the result of powerful mystical experiences.[186] I explore just this issue in a paper entitled *Mystical Experience and Global Revolution*.[187] In that paper I marshal an argument suggesting that the transformative potential of mystical experience is what will save the world. And fundamental transformation is what is required, and fast. A recent editorial in the *Monthly Review* acknowledges what I have been talking about in this whole essay, which is that we face a global economic and ecological crisis of apocalyptic proportions, a crisis caused by the Family's regime of accumulation. The editors suggest that if we are to save humanity we need fundamental revolutionary change.

> Indeed, so great is the epochal crisis of our time; encompassing both the economic and ecological crises, that nothing but a world revolution is likely to save humanity (and countless others among the earths' species) from a worsening series of catastrophes.[188]

---

[186] I myself accomplished a fundamental revision in my atheist views and values over a decade ago when I experienced what I would now characterize as strong (but initially brief) connections to the Fabric of Consciousness. I talk more about that first (of many) mystical experiences in Sharp, *Lightning Path Book One - Introduction to the Lightning Path*, 1.

[187] Mike Sosteric, "Mystical Experience and Global Revolution," *Athens Journal of Social Sciences* (2018).

[188] Editorial, "Notes from the Editors," *The Monthly Review* 66, no. 1 (2014).

The editors of *Monthly Review* are calling for revolutionary political change, but for reasons already enumerated, I believe that any form of permanent change to the material conditions we live under must start with revolutionary change to our archetypes, consciousness, and values. That in turn requires, in addition to some serious archetypal revision, mystical experience, or as I prefer, global connection to The Fabric. To be as clear as possible, *only a rapid and massive global evolution of values and an equally rapid and massive expansion of consciousness, both caused by a global re-connection to The Fabric (i.e. mystical experience), is what will save the world.* And once again, I am not the only one to suggest the importance of mystical experience. Albert Einstein himself suggested that a total absence of religion would lead to "incalculable harm to human progress."[189] Einstein felt it was religion, stripped of its primitive anthropomorphisms by the purifying

---

[189] Albert Einstein, *Out of My Later Years*(Citadel Press, 2000). Also included in an interesting collection by Nancy K. Frankenberry, *The Faith of Scientists in Their Own Words*(New Jersey: Princeton University Press, 2008), 163.

actions of science,[190] that could "liberate mankind... from the bondage of egocentric cravings, desires, and fears."[191]

To be sure, Einstein can be a bit obtuse on the whole issue. Harvey, on the other hand, is quite clear on the significance of mystical connection. As he notes:

> There is nothing more important... for the future of the planet — than an authentic and unsparing recovery of the full range, power, and glory of ... mystical tradition. Without such a recovery, the spiritual life of the West will continue to be a superficial, narcissistic, and sometimes lethal mixture of a watered-down or fanatical pseudo-Christianity; hardly understood "Eastern" metaphysics and regressive occultism—and the great radical potential of such a renaissance will go unlived and unenacted with disastrous consequences for every human being and for all of nature.

Harvey suggests that it is "Christian mystical tradition" that will save the planet, but I have to disagree. There may be something in Christian mystical tradition that is valuable, but there are lots of mystical traditions in the East and West that may provide insight as well. And besides, as I note above, the guidance of Christianity (like the mystical

---

[190] Einstein felt that if religion was to play its part in bringing about progressive change for humanity, "teachers of religion" would have to "give up the doctrine of a personal God" and "avail themselves of those forces which are capable of cultivating the Good, the True, and the Beautiful in humanity itself." See Albert Einstein, "Science and Religion," in *The Conference on Science, Philosophy and Religion In Their Relation to the Democratic Way of Life, Inc.*(New York1941).

[191] *Ideas and Opinions*(Broadway Books, 1995).

guidance of all traditions) may be too obscured, obfuscated, and dated to be of much use. Therefore, we may need something new.[192] Still, I do whole heartedly agree with Harvey that authentic mystical experience, or as I would say, connection to The Fabric, will make the difference between a violent descent into political and environmental chaos and destruction, and the transformation and salvation of the world.

BRINGING SCIENCE ON BOARD

The above appeal to take mystical experience seriously is sincere; however, the science oriented individual may yet resist. In this regard, a misplaced faith in science's ability to solve world problems may be at the root. To put it bluntly, it may be hard to take religion seriously given how "successful" science has been at moving us all forward. Science has brought technology, increased production, advanced medicine, and a long list of amazing advances. Because of science's technological success, secular humanists often put the same kind of blind faith in science that others put in religion and salvation. Unfortunately, blind faith in science as salvation, a blind-faith aptly documented by David Noble,[193] is misplaced. Back in 1988 David Griffin edited a collection of articles entitled *The*

---

[192] I am in the process of developing this "something new". I call it *The Lightning Path* and it is a spiritual pathway designed to teach an authentic spirituality facilitated by mystical experience and spiritual awakening. For more information, visit http://www.lightningpath.org/

[193] David Noble, *The Religion of Technology: The Divinity of Man and the Spirit of Invention*(New York: Penguin, 1999).

Re-enchantment of Science.[194] In this collection, scientists bemoaned the state of the earth. They pointed to "planetary difficulties" like nuclear warheads, ecocide, and global inequality, and said, in a rather forthright statement, that science, or rather scientists, were to blame. The problem was manifold. From a meaningless and empty mechanism (the disenchantment of science as Griffin called it), to a failure of story-telling,[195] to simple lack of faith in their own abilities (a lack of faith that it turns out even Einstein was victim of),[196] science had done something terribly wrong, and the world was descending into the pit as a result.

Twenty-five years later it is hard not to agree with their original assessment because the world has clearly descended further into the pit. We only have to look out the window and see the weather these days to know that something is horribly wrong with the planet. Beyond that, the growing gap between rich and poor, the growing concentration of wealth, the global collapse of alternative politics, the global domination of destructive accumulation regimes, the concomitant destruction of the environment, growing violence and chaos, and the imminent collapse of the global job market caused by the rapid development of automated technology like self-driving cars, paint a totally dystopian picture. Scott Santens, for example, draws out

[194] David Ray Griffin, "Introduction: The Reenchantment of Science," in *The Reenchantment of Science*, ed. David Ray Griffin(New York: State University of New York, 1988).

[195] Brian Swimme, "The Cosmic Creation Story," ibid.

[196] David Bohm, "Postmodern Science and a Postmodern World," ibid.

the negative economic and human implications for the rapid emergence of self-driving trucks, and it isn't pretty.[197] Massive economic disruption caused by companies looking to ramp up accumulation by eliminating pesky, expensive humans is just around the corner. And they are going to do it. Companies like Uber, despite their sometimes lofty rhetoric of global transformation and human interest, are driven by nothing more than their desire to get in on the accumulation bandwagon. They don't care about humans, they don't care of the economic struggle of nations, and they don't care if the world crashes around them. They only care that they can increase their rates of accumulation. Travis Kalanick, the founder of Uber, said he will replace human drivers with technology without batting an eyelid.

> You're not just paying for the car — you're paying for the other dude in the car," he said. "When there's no other dude in the car, the cost of taking an Uber anywhere becomes cheaper than owning a vehicle." That, he said, will "bring the cost below the cost of ownership for everybody, and then car ownership goes away.[198]

Whole industries, entire economies, and in fact the fabric of the entire world is on the brink of an imminent

---

[197] Stott Santens draws out the negative economic and human implications for the rapid emergence of self-driving trucks, and it isn't pretty. Massive economic disruption caused by companies looking to ramp up accumulation by eliminating pesky, expensive, humans is arguably just around the corner.

[198] Kalanick is quoted by Emily Guendelsberger, "I Was an Undercover Uber Driver," *Philadelphia City Paper* 2015.

economic implosion caused by the intersection of light-speed technology and out of control accumulation, and science is definitely culpable here. Not only has science provided the (surveillance, military, productive, and psychological) technology to control the masses, wipe out jobs, increase accumulation, and destroy the planet,[199] but science has also provided the moral and ethical void that makes it possible to do just that. As Griffin and the rest of the authors in his collection convey, scientists have deliberately written purpose, meaning, feeling, experiences, and ideals out of its precious equations. I would go further and say that scientists, despite the appeals of heavy weights like Einstein, have emptied the cosmos of spirituality, consciousness, and divinity and left a hopeless world of hopeless and confused people who seem unable to do anything but stand and wait for the increasingly obvious and inevitable crash.

To be fair, David Griffin and the scientists in his book did propose solutions.[200] They suggested we re-sacrilize science,

---

[199] James Beniger provides an enlightening look at the Family's expanding capacity to *control* everything on the planet. His analysis was stunning back in 1989 and that was before modern communication and smart-phone technologies tied everybody so thoroughly into the same global surveillance network. See James R Beniger, *The Control Revolution: Technological and Economic Origins of the Information Society* (Boston: Harvard University Press, 1989).

[200] Also to be fair, it was Auguste Comte, the founding father of sociology, who was the first (by a long shot) to suggest the need to keep the sacred in science. Auguste even set out to develop a scientifically aligned religion called *The Catechism of Positivism.* In my opinion his attempt, while laudable, failed for the same

recognize our own limitations, return to essentials (i.e. basic search for truth), admit to the "nonecological" and reductionist assumptions of our theories and methods, and even engage in some serious story telling in order to create better foundations for a more situated and sensible science. But twenty-five years later things have not gotten better at all. Despite the existence of the oddball heretic here and there, science is as spiritually dead as it ever was and as a result, our decline into global chaos and catastrophe has accelerated in an increasingly exponential fashion.

So, what's the problem? Well, the problem is that scientists, even sympathetic ones, have missed the point. They may have tried to re-enchant science, but like Swimme's strained and painful attempt to construct an enchanting cosmology,[201] they have failed miserably because they refuse to think beyond the little materialist corner into which they have painted themselves, except perhaps in the most simplistic and spiritually immature ways. They try to develop new world views and new perspectives; they speak of wholeness and enfoldment,[202] they connect empirical anomalies in the material world to

---

reason that attempts like Griffin have failed, i.e. a refusal to think beyond the materialist box. Auguste Comte, *The Catechism of Positivism; or, Summary Exposition of the Universal Religion*(London: John Chapman, 1852).

[201] Swimme, "The Cosmic Creation Story." For my own attempt to "re-enchant" the world with a modern creation story, see Sharp, *The Song of Creation: The Story of Genesis*.

[202] David Bohm, *Wholeness and the Implicate Order*(London: Routledge Kegan Paul, 1980).

morphic fields;[203] but, they struggle to find new stories because they leave the universe empty of the most important thing of all, God[204] (or what I call the *Fabric of Consciousness*). Some scientists may be willing to consider

---

[203] Rupert Sheldrake, *Morphic Resonance: The Nature of Formative Causatoin*(Rochester, Vermont: Inner Traditions, 2009).

[204] **God, God, God?** Let me just get this out of the way right now and say that *there is not a single word in any language that has more baggage than the word "God"*. Say the word "God" and definitions and images instantly come to mind. And the knee-jerk reaction isn't always positive. People have visceral, reactive, and sometimes even violently negative reactions when that word is mentioned. Some people hear the word "God" used and they shutdown, shut off, and stop listening, often assuming a definition before even trying to understand what is meant by the term. So let me tell you that when I, as a mystic, use the word "God" I absolutely do not mean some beard baring patriarch in the sky. My conception of God is rooted in my direct mystical experiences *and* my scientific exploration of said mystical experience, and that tells me that God is about as far from that personalized, patriarchal image that some people have as human beings are from the one cell amoeba. Of course, saying this doesn't mean God is not a personal consciousness. God is as personal as you and I. In fact, as many mystics, including Jesus Christ, have said, God is you and I(!) so God is as personal as you and I choose to be.

I keep a collection of quotes from mystics like Christ, Mohammed, Kabir, and so on to support this basic position. You can visit it at https://www.michaelsharp.org/who-am-i/.

I explicate the nature of God and Consciousness in Sharp, *The Book of Light: The Nature of God, the Structure of Consciousness, and the Universe within You*, one -air.

a re-enchantment, but because they are locked inside a little materialist box they miss the proverbial spiritual boat. They cannot do it because they leave out the one thing (The Fabric/Consciousness/God) that must, because of its essential reality, be at the core of any re-enchantment attempt.

So what are we, as scientists, to do? To be blunt, we have to give up our precious materialism and consider another option. If we really want to give science the push it needs, we have to consider the heresy (what amounts to a *fact* in my view) that there is "something more" that exists independently of material creation. It is this "more" that is what we should be looking for, and looking at, and it is this more that will help us re-enchant science and save the world.

Now, I can understand if the idea of bringing "more" back into science bothers you a bit, especially if you are a scientist. After all, all scientists *know* that there is nothing more. The universe begins and ends with what we can see, and that's the bottom line! As for spirituality and religion, that is mere superstition. We, as scientists, just do not go for that kind of thing. We all know that our colleagues are generally hostile towards spirituality and religion.[205] We all know that our colleagues think that spirituality and religion are irrational holdouts from a more intellectually primitive

---

[205] See for example Rodney Stark, "On the Incompatibility of Religion and Science: A Survey of American Graduate Students," *Journal for the Scientific Study of Religion* 3, no. 1 (1963): 3; Richard Featherstone and Katie Sorrell, "Sociology Dismissing Religion? The Presentation of Religious Change in Introductory Sociology Textbooks," *American Sociologist* 38, no. 1 (2007).

time. As such, as scientists, we naturally battle religion in a bitter fight to end the delusion. This battle with irrational religion, which we think is going on, is refracted into the public eye by people like Richard Dawkins[206] who carry it forward. The net result is that everybody (scientists and lay people alike) assume that scientists are atheists and that they reject religion and spirituality outright. As Ecklund and Long note:

> Scholars and public intellectuals almost uniformly perceive scientists as the carriers of a secularist impulse, a group responsible for building the modern research university and undermining religious authority by their success in deciphering the mysteries of the natural order without recourse to supernatural aid or guidance.[207]

"We are scientists, we are scientists, we are scientists," we cry, and therefore we cannot brook the notion that there may be something more. Everybody knows that to the secular, rational scientist, this "more" is anathema pure and simple.

Or so we have been led to believe.

The problem with this view of scientists as secular atheists is that it is just not true. The cracks in this hegemonic edifice appeared earlier when we discussed mystical experience and demonstrated how a few prominent scientists took mystical experience seriously. The cracks turn into crumbling blocks of concrete when we consider recent research which has demonstrated that *most*

---

[206] Dawkins, *The God Delusion.*

[207] Ecklund and Long, "Scientists and Spirituality," 254.

scientists are *spiritual.* Ecklund and Long sent a survey out to the top scientists in the top universities and asked them if they were spiritual. The answer was an unequivocal yes! Ecklund and Long say it quite clearly: "Our results show unexpectedly that the majority of scientists at top research universities consider themselves 'spiritual....'"[208] But hold your breath, it gets better! Taking the iconoclastic research a step further, Ecklund and Long note that rather than being naturally hostile to spiritual exploration, in fact scientists are naturally spiritual! Spirituality is, according to the authors of the study, part of who we are.

> For many scientists, spirituality meshes beautifully with their identities as scientists because they also see spirituality as an individual journey, as a quest for meanings that can never be final, just as is the case for scientific explanations of reality.... For some their sense of spirituality flows very deeply from the work that they do as scientists.[209]

In other words, spirituality is an extension of the scientist's already powerful drive for truth.

I can certainly concur with this because it fits my experience exactly. Although I wasn't always a spiritual person, in fact for a long time I was an avowed atheist, now I am a very spiritual person. And I am not a spiritual person based on stupidity, irrationality, or delusion, as someone like Richard Dawkins may want you to believe. My spirituality emerged out of two things. On the one hand it emerged out of actual spiritual experience (i.e. I have had

---

[208] Ibid., 255.: emphasis added

[209] Ibid., 262.

many mystical connections to the Fabric of Consciousness). On the other hand, it arises out of a human drive to seek the truth, a drive Abraham Maslow argued is a fundamental part of our human structure of needs.[210] To be as succinct as possible, I became spiritual not because of some delusionary belief or primitive and irrational longing. *I became spiritual* when I had experiences that could not be explained within the rubric of a materialist worldview, and I was driven, by basic human instinct, to figure it all out.[211] It was mystical experience coupled with a basic cognitive need to know and understand that altered my atheism and drew me forward on a spiritual path of exploration and analysis.

> Mystical connection led me to experience things not compatible with materialism; science led to search for the truth about those experiences.

I do not want to get into a long-winded discussion of the spirituality of scientists or my own work on mysticism and spirituality. To end this essay, I'll just say, as Einstein and

---

[210] In his seminal 1943 article, Abraham Maslow argued that humans have fundamental and powerful cognitive *need to know and understand.* He suggested that this need to know drives us to answer the big questions. As I argue in an article entitled *What is Religion,* it is these powerful cognitive needs that underpin religion and drive us all on an eternal quest for truth, with a capital "T".

See Maslow, "A Theory of Human Motivation." Also see Michael Sosteric, "What Is Religion?," *The Socjourn* 2015.

[211] I tell the story of my mystical experiences in the chapter on *Origins* in Sharp, *Lightning Path Book One - Introduction to the Lightning Path,* 1.

others have said, that spirituality is compatible with science and, as recent research has demonstrated, most scientists have no problem with having the two in the same room. And this is a good thing. Einstein clearly saw religion and science as compatible, complementary, and dependent on each other. On the one hand, science was dependent on religion because religion provided the orientation, i.e. (the enchanting cosmology) and the "untiring devotion" that drove the scientist's search for the deep truths of nature.[212] On the other hand, religion was dependent on science because science "purifies the religious impulse of the dross of its anthropomorphism [and] contributes to a religious

―――――――――――――――――

[212] Perhaps his clearest statement on the issue comes in a 1948 article he wrote for the *Christian Register*

> The interpretation of religion, as here advanced, implies a dependence of science on the religious attitude, a relation which, in our predominantly materialistic age, is only too easily overlooked. While it is true that scientific results are entirely independent from religious or moral considerations, those individuals to whom we owe the great creative achievements of science were all of them imbued with the truly religious conviction that this universe of ours is something perfect and susceptible to the rational striving for knowledge. If this conviction had not been a strongly emotional one and if those searching for knowledge had not been inspired by Spinoza's *Amor Dei Intellectualis*, they would hardly have been capable of that untiring devotion which alone enables man to attain his greatest achievements.

See Albert Einstein, "Religion and Science: Irreconcilable?," *The Christian Register* (1948).

spiritualization of our understanding of life."[213] In other words, religion helped sacralise science, something that Einstein and others see as essential, and science helped rationalize religion by making the pursuit and revelation of the "rationality made manifest in existence" the primary goal of scientific endeavour.[214]

According to Einstein, the two are compatible and it is past time we brought them together in the same room. Of course, this does not mean the two are unproblematically compatible. I would be the first to admit that there are some major problems with traditional religions as they currently sit, not the least of which is that they are often exploited by elites to control the masses, and thus they often do everything but discuss and teach about the authentic core. When was the last time you heard a priest or guru telling you that you had to explore mystical

---

[213] Ibid.

[214] "Science and Religion."

I should note that Einstein had no respect for the personalized patriarch of religion. While he did feel that religion was the best hope for humanity because it was religion that could help humanity transcend the "competitive spirit", he did not brook a personalized patriarch and felt that this was nothing more than a solace accessible to the "undeveloped mind". In his own word:

> Nobody, certainly, will deny that the idea of the existence of an omnipotent, just, and omnibeneficent personal God is able to accord man solace, help, and guidance; also, by virtue of its simplicity it is accessible to the most undeveloped mind.

Ibid.

experience to be a spiritual person? While I think there is potential in spirituality, I also think that control of religion has to be wrested from people who exploit it for their own venal interests. If spirituality and religion are to fulfil the potential that I, Einstein, and others attribute to it, the authentic core will have to uncovered/recovered and authentic teachings will have to be distributed to the planet.[215]

In closing this chapter, I just want to conclude by saying this. Given everything that has been said so far, a defensive and hostile posture that rejects the exploration of spirituality and mystical experience is untenable and ridiculous. This is so not only because scientists do in fact believe in something more, not only because scientists think about the issues, not only because science and the "religious impulse" are compatible, even instinctual, but primarily because, as I would argue, time is running out and mysticism and authentic connection may be the best hope for humanity. Accumulation regimes, regimes we (as scientists) have helped create, and which we currently support with our intellectual work and research,[216] have

---

[215] Recovering the authentic core is something that I am attempting to do with my *Lightning Path* system of spiritual teachings. Visit http://www.lightningpath.org for more information.

[216] For an early critical take on the contribution of the social sciences to the Family's regime of accumulation, see Robin Blackburn, *Ideology in Social Science: Readings in Critical Theory*(Glasgow: Fontana, 1975). For a look at the conservative roots of early American Sociology, see Martin Nicolaus, "The Professional Organization of Sociology: A View from Below," in

created an environmentally, socially, psychologically, and spiritually destructive system that has brought us all to the brink. Without a fundamental change in values caused by a collective and authentic mystical awakening, life as most of us know it will be over, and the human species as it currently exists will not survive.

And do not kid yourself. All the cool technological toys that technology brings isn't going to save us, it is going to sink us faster. We either put aside our prejudice, shift our focus, put aside the Family's ideological corruptions, support massive global value change, and take a serious look at the mystical side of things (a side which, as I note above and in the article Dangerous Memories,[217] provides the foundation for the rapid transformation that is required), or we continue to circle the proverbial, world ending drain. It is our choice, but we have to make it quick because we are all running out of time.

Ideology in Social Science: Readings in Critical Social Theory, ed. Robin Blackburn(Glasgow: Fontana, 1975).

[217] Sosteric, "Mystical Experience and Global Revolution."

CONCLUSION:
GETTING THE FAMILY ON BOARD

> Just 62 people, 53 of them men, own as much wealth as the poorest half of the entire world population and the richest 1 percent own more than the other 99 percent put together.[218]

This brings us to an end of this short, but diverse, essay. We started our journey by looking at money and ended it by making an appeal to global mystical religious experience. Between those remarkable extremes we have discussed accumulation, debt, global economic crisis, growing ecological catastrophe, the importance of mystical connection, scientific prejudice, and so on. That's quite the traverse, but the rhyme and reason should be easy to see at this point. The goal of this book has been to identify the problem and suggest a solution. The problem is, accumulation regimes are destroying the world. The solution is, end the Regime. How we do that seems relatively straight forward. To end the accumulation regimes that are destroying this world we need to ...

a) Educate the population about the true nature of money (which we can do with this essay),

b) Repudiate debt to free up necessary resources.

c) Root out old energy archetypes that provide ideological support for violence and exploitation and replace them with new energy archetypes.

---

[218] Quoted in Ben Hirschler and Noah Barkin, "A World Divided: Elites Descend on Swiss Alps Amid Rising Inequality," *Reuters News Wire* 2016.

d) Change consciousness, values, and priorities by healing the damage done by toxic socialization, and by pursuing a necessary global mysticism.

e) Eliminate the accumulation regime that is causing such horrible global suffering and rapidly destroying the entire planet.

To be sure, these are difficult challenges and they will require massive amounts of intense and concentrated effort and work, but we need to do the work. Collectively we stand at the cusp of a golden age. Science and technology is rapidly advancing. Intractable diseases are starting to fall by the way side and 3D printing is evolving so rapidly that printing human organs is becoming a real possibility.[219] Indeed, some very rich people are also starting to talk about the possibility of curing death![220] More realistic for many perhaps, we certainly have the productive and technological expertise to house the planet, connect the people, and end world hunger. We also have the resources and, as advanced technologies begin to replace human labor in many industries, an available army of labor power with which to do it. What we need is an end to the regime, a shift in global priorities, and a release of global funds currently accumulated in the hands of only a few people. If we could accomplish this shift in priorities and this release of funds, surely we would not have difficulty stopping the slide into global chaos.

---

[219] Dylan Love, "Researchers in Kentucky Are Trying to 3d Print a Working Human Heart out of Fat Cells," *Business Insider* 2014.

[220] Harry McCracken, "Google Vs. Death," *Time* 2013.

This might seem like a tall order, but you should certainly feel motivated and empowered with the potential to achieve the goal. With modern communication technology (i.e. the Internet, the WWW, smartphones, etc.) such as it is, we could easily educate the population and get everything aligned just perfectly within only a few years. The problem is, one obstacle stands in our way and that obstacle is the Family. The problem is after centuries of accumulation, the Family own and control everything. A case in point is the failed "Occupy Wall Street" movement. They (or their upper and middle management reps) own all the media, control all the technology, run all governments and the corporations, direct all military and police technology, and generally are able to do whatever they want, whenever they feel like it. They have accumulated trillions of hours of labor power and all that accumulated labor gives them ultimate power. The World Wide Web has given some reprieve by allowing everybody else on the planet to communicate and share outside of the media box we usually live within, but with their money and resources it is probably only a matter of time before they exert enough legislative and technical control over the Internet to eliminate its progressive potential. In this regard it is noteworthy that a single corporate big brother, Google, controls over 90% of search engine traffic.[221] And if this doesn't scare you, it should. Every website you find comes to you because Google recommended it. This wouldn't be a problem if Google provided a transparent view of the Internet, but they don't. Google works very hard to control

---

[221] "How Much Search Traffic Actually Comes from Googling? ," eMarketer, http://www.emarketer.com/Article/How-Much-Search-Traffic-Actually-Comes-Googling/1011814.

what you see and they don't bother to tell anybody how they are doing it. They use algorithms that let "quality" sites (as defined exclusively by Google) higher into the search listings, and these same algorithms push "lower quality sites" (also as defined exclusively by Google) lower. Since most people never view links past the first page of search results, this effectively obscures any website that Google doesn't want you to see!

You may choose to view Google as a benevolent behemoth or as the modern day incarnation of George Orwell's Big Brother but regardless of your view, the reality is Google's activities make or break a public website. One cleaning service in Dallas Texas was broken by Google's ongoing efforts to "refine" search results. This company, called Golden Services, had been signing up one to two new customers a day but "traffic plunged overnight after Google's algorithm change. New sign-ups fell to about one to two a week and the company cut its staff to four from nine... A search on 'house cleaning service' and 'Frisco, Texas,' where [the] company is based, buries the site around the third page of listings, even though it lands high in results on Google Maps."[222] And it is not just small business and alternative websites that may suffer. Global democracy may take a *fatal* hit as well! In a study published in the *Proceedings of the National Academy of Sciences*,[223]

---

[222] Ari Levi, "Has Google Lost Control of Its Anti-Spam Algorithm," AlleyWatch, http://www.alleywatch.com/2015/09/google-lost-control-anti-spam-algorithm/.

[223] Robert Epstein and Ronald E. Robertson, "The Search Engine Manipulation Effect (Seme) and Its Possible Impact on the

Epstein and Robertson found what they call the *Search Engine Manipulation Effect* (or SEME). According to the scientists, the SEME is the "largest behavioral effect ever discovered." Reporting on their research in Politico magazine, Epstein says:

> Our new research leaves little doubt about whether Google has the ability to control voters. In laboratory and online experiments conducted in the United States, we were able to boost the proportion of people who favored any candidate by between 37 and 63 percent after just one search session. The impact of viewing biased rankings repeatedly over a period of weeks or months would undoubtedly be larger. [224]

They also note that "given that many elections are won by small margins, this gives Google the power, right now, to flip upwards of 25 percent of the national elections worldwide." This is a remarkable statement. Never in the history of the world have so few people (a handful of executives and engineers at Google) had so much power over global politics. Google reaches into the homes and work places of every citizen in every country on the planet with the ability to manipulate thought. That is an unprecedented, and largely unacknowledged, global influence.

What is even more disturbing, the authors of the study suggest that Google may have already determined the

---

Outcomes of Elections," *Proceedings of the National Academy of Sciences* 112, no. 33 (2015).

[224] Robert Epstein, "How Google Could Rig the 2016 Election," Politico, www.politico.com/magazine/story/2015/08/how-google-could-rig-the-2016-election-121548.

outcome of a recent election in India by influencing search results and seating a conservative client! Here is a summary of their conclusions in their own words:

> Given how powerful this effect is, it's possible that Google decided the winner of the Indian election. Google's own daily data on election-related search activity (subsequently removed from the Internet, but not before my colleagues and I downloaded the pages) showed that Narendra Modi, the ultimate winner, outscored his rivals in search activity by more than 25 percent for sixty-one consecutive days before the final votes were cast. That high volume of search activity could easily have been generated by higher search rankings for Modi.

The moral of the story here is that information technology gives the Family incredible control over the minds and hearts of the people. Of course "we" (and by "we" I mean all the people at the bottom of the hill) might be able to push the pendulum a bit if we struggle hard enough. After all, we can all build websites and distribute our own alternative articles through social media; but unfortunately, we do not have the time left to struggle or the resources to deal with the resistance. Saving the planet requires immediate and rapid changes starting right now. Given the ultimate power that the Family has, the only way that this is going to happen is if the Family and their supporters either suddenly (or over the course of a few years) drop dead, or they all get on the mystical value-change bandwagon with everybody else. The question is, will they get on board?

Certainly there are moves in that direction. Warren Buffet, one of the richest men on the planet, admits the existence of a class war between the Family and everybody else.[225] Perhaps recognizing his culpability, he has more recently called for an extremely modest tax increase for the wealthy.[226] Even more radical perhaps, some of the world's richest people have signed a "Giving Pledge"[227] where they promise to give away all, or at least a substantial portion, of their wealth. But even if Bill and Melinda Gates and the rest of the world's billionaires give away their money in a Kumbaya type pledge, it won't be enough. Giving away wealth is just a band aid solution. It is simply another desperate attempt to reset the economy, while soothing guilt and salving conscience. It is not going to work because it leaves the Family firmly in control and the System firmly in place. With the Family in control and the System in place, the logic of accumulation, debt, growth, and consumerism would remain. With the System in place it will only be a matter of time before the global ecology and economy collapses. The only thing that is going to work is what I have already suggested.

a) Educate the population about the true nature of money (which we can do with this essay),

b) Repudiate debt to free up necessary resources.

---

[225] Ben Stein, *In Class Warfare, Guess Which Class Is Winning*, vol. September(New York Times, 2006).

[226] Warren E. Buffet, "A Minimum Tax for the Wealthy," *New York Times*2012.

[227] The Giving Pledge is a commitment by the world's wealthiest individual to give away the majority of their wealth. You can see the smiling faces of all the "noble" and "magnanimous" givers making the pledge by visiting the Giving Pledge website http://givingpledge.org.

c) Root out old energy archetypes that provide ideological support for violence and exploitation and replace them with new energy archetypes.
d) Change consciousness, values, and priorities by healing the damage done by toxic socialization, and by pursuing a necessary global mysticism.
e) Eliminate the accumulation regime that is causing such horrible global suffering and rapidly destroying the entire planet.

Everything else is just an attempt to re-dress the department store window.

So, what is the next move? Well, given the arguably valid statement that we need the Family to get on board so we can change the world real fast, we basically need to encourage the Family to get on board the boat with the rest of us! It is not impossible. There are a few things that I can think of to do and I'm sure you can think of some more as well.

For one, you need to control your anger and resentment. Do not be hostile towards the Family. Do not judge, or threaten to punish. Do not wave sticks, do not throw stones, and do not build guillotines. In other words, do not give the Family any reason to fear the consequences of letting go. If you act like an angry mob, the Family is not going to get on the lifeboat even if their ship has sunk! This is not about good gathering into armies to beat down evil, this is about joining together to save the planet. If the Family thinks that getting on board is going to lead to emotional, psychological, or physical pain and suffering, they are not going to do it. And who can blame them? Only a fool is going to willingly put themselves into a position where they know they are going to experience, suffering, violence, and abuse (euphemistically referred to as "punishment"). And besides, for all the pain and suffering that the Family has caused, we still have to admit things are [technologically] better now than they were a thousand years ago. They have had a part in this development, so give credit where credit is due. We should thank the Family for the work they have done in helping to build the technological marvel that is our modern world and forgive them their trespasses so they can more easily jump on the lifeboat and devote their resources to real change.

Two, we need to educate the Family just like we need to educate everybody else. Judging by the self-assured and congratulatory back slapping of the recent Paris conference on climate change, they may think they know how to save the world; but even if a miracle happened and all the world nations suddenly agreed to changes beyond the insufficient "achievements" of the Paris conference, it won't be enough. There is no nice way to say this, but they are all limited by their greed, avarice, spiritual ignorance, and unwillingness to let go of their wealth and power. Because of that (and some other reasons I won't get into here), they (and by "they" I mean rich Family members the world over) operate within a *very* narrow range of possibilities. At their current spiritual level, any solutions they come up with will be designed with continuity of their regime of accumulation in mind. Of course, they may deny that, and you may be tempted to believe them, especially when they publically pat themselves on the back for what a wonderful job they are doing, or dress up their denials with Hollywood high production value, but don't buy the BS.

Putting a little green technology forward, or leveling off greenhouse gas emissions, is not going to save the planet. The only thing that is going to save the planet is the elimination of the accumulation regime that is destroying it. If the planet is going to be saved, the System cannot continue, period. Therefore, we need to persistently and insistently point out that the old systems are crumbling and the toxic climate it has created is ruinous to all. It may take a while to get the message through their ideological defense mechanisms, but it will get through. It has to. All the money in the world will not make them immune from the changes that are coming. Given the increasingly sorry state of the world, they do not have a choice but to listen, wake up, and make change. If they do not they are going to die in the ensuing violence, chaos, and ecological collapse just like everybody else.

Three, and finally, lead by example. If you want the Family to change, heck if you want your own family to change, lead by example. Do the right thing and then show that off to the world. And do not be modest or shy about it. If things are going to change, we need behavioral leaders to exhibit to the world. This is important. As any psychologist will tell you, humans learn by seeing and modelling the behavior of others, so don't be shy. Model good behavior to your children, to your coworkers, to the Family, and everyone.[228] I know some readers might think this is hopelessly naïve, but there are good neuro-biological reasons to emphasize this as at least part of a plan of solution. Our human primate brain is loaded with what neuroscientists call mirror neurons. Mirror neurons, which Acharya and

---

[228] There are a lot of ways to do this. You could even start your

Shukla say are one of the "most important discoveries in the last decade of neuroscience", are a subset of brain neurons that fire in sympathetic response to "actions that we observe in others"[229] These neurons were discovered in research with macaque monkeys where researchers found that motor neurons in the monkey's brain fired when the monkey's simply watched experimenters engage an action.[230] For example, when an experimenter picked up a peanut, the same motor neurons fired in the monkey brain that fired when the monkeys themselves picked up a peanut! In other words, the simple act of watching another engage an action was neurobiologically identical to engaging the action for oneself. In other words, the external reality that the monkey was watching was impacting and even changing the monkey brain itself.

Since the publication of the original study, motor neurons have been linked to human learning, bursts of human evolution[231] and even human empathy.[232] These are

---

[229] Sourya Acharya and Samarth Shukla, "Mirror Neurons: Enigma of the Metaphysical Modular Brain," *Journal of Natural Science, Biology, and Medicine* 3, no. 2 (2012): 118..

[230] G. Rizzolatti, L. Fogassi, and V. Gallese, "Neurophysiological Mechanisms Underlying the Understanding and Imitation of Action," *Nat Rev Neurosci* 2, no. 9 (2001).

[231] V.S. Ramachandran, "Mirror Neurons and Imitation Learning as the Driving Force Behind "the Great Leap Forward" in Human Evolution," Edge, http://edge.org/3rd_culture/ramachandran/ramachandran_index.html.,

[232] Bruno Wicker et al., "Both of Us Disgusted in My Insula," *Neuron* 40, no. 3.

plausible, intuitively reasonable, and psychologically established connections. Psychologists have known forever, or at least since Albert Bandura published his *Bobo Doll* experiments where he demonstrated that human children would beat up a clown doll if they saw adults beating it up first,[233] that humans learn and model the activity of the adults that surround them. The discovery of motor neurons only adds a neurobiological foundation for what has been known for decades, which is that we all have a responsibility and a duty to act nice towards each other. If we want people to become less greedy, less competitive, less materialistic, and more spiritually advanced, we must model this. Note that I don't recommend you go out and buy crystal and singing bowls and sing Kumbaya, because that will make you the brunt of jokes, but you can talk about new ways of thinking around a dinner table, model news of behaving, and even watch a documentary or two on new ways of looking at the world. If you make your life less about the materialist pursuit of wealth in a global competitive environment and more about daily transformation and spiritual evolution, others will do the same.

Of course, as important as individual action within your own family is, it is going to take a lot more than just talk around a dinner table and actions with your own family. Our current media universe is saturated with acts of physical, social, and psychological violence. On a daily basis we see violence and this violence fires our mirror neurons and helps re-create the world we live in. If our

---

[233] A Bandura, *Social Learning and Personality Development*(New York: Hold, Rinehart & Winston, 1963).

brains mirror and transform in line with what we see in the world, and if mirror neurons really did facilitate previous evolutionary leaps as Ramachandran suggests,[234] then Hollywood, television, and other forms of media which show us unending streams of violence, conflict, struggle, and horror are leading us down a path of devolution and destruction. If witnessing violence changes our brains and the world, we have a real problem. Hollywood has always been big on violence, destruction, good bashing evil, and revenge; but these days they seem only capable of turning a buck on duality, conflict, and violence. This is particularly true now that special effects and CGI have made it possible to materialize any image that enters the fevered mind of the writer. With the emergence of studios like Marvel, and the total lack of imagination now being presented to us on Hollywood screens,[235] the domination of consciousness by images that support violence and exploitation is complete. There is no alternative. Even so called reality television is a construction and presentation of greed and violence. Indeed, reality television presents "extremely high levels of aggression, of up to 84.67 times an hour".[236] These shows "idolize" and reward social competition, deceit,

---

[234] Wicker et al., "Both of Us Disgusted in My Insula."

[235] It is notable that two recent blockbusters, Jurassic World and Star Wars The Force Awakens, where nothing but gussied up versions of movies written 30 years ago! Hollywood's imagination is in the gutter, gutter, gutter.

[236] Sarah M. Coyne, Simon L. Robinson, and David A. Nelson, "Does Reality Backbite? Physical, Verbal, and Relational Aggression in Reality Television Programs," *Journal of Broadcasting & Electronic Media* 54, no. 2 (2010).

"blindsides", and other forms of social violence and aggression. In the words of one college student, reality television presents "lying and deceit...instead of ... goodwill and friendly competition".[237]

Given the salience of motor neurons and modelling, this is going to have to change. Media moguls from Fox to YouTube are going to have to stop using their power to present images of violence, competition, stupidity,[238] greed, and abuse of power, and start presenting images of cooperation, goodwill, and social responsibility. The gut reaction here may be "well that's going to be boring", but that's not true. There was a time when Hollywood was far more socially informed and critical than it is now. The classic 70s sitcom *All in the Family* was all about educating the masses about racism and intolerance, and recent examples like the sci-fi classic *Firefly* demonstrate that ethics, morality, and good behavior can be presented in entertaining vehicles. And there are alternatives besides violence and destruction. Movies like *The Last Mimzy* present images of spiritual evolution and ascendant consciousness and it is possible to envision other formulas for television dramas with the same imagery and intent. I myself have worked on a script for a television series designed to present new energy archetypes and a spiritually evolving planet, rather than the constant gush of dystopian

---

[237] Lisa K. Lundy, Amanda M. Ruth, and Travis D. Park, "Simply Irresistible: Reality Tv Consumption Patterns," *Communication Quarterly* 56, no. 2 (2008).

[238] I won't name any names, but some of the richest moguls on YouTube got that way by simply being stupid on camera.

violence we see.[239] This script may be a hack, but it demonstrates the possibility. The problem is the Family. It takes a lot of money and talent to develop and produce a script and right now Hollywood is controlled by a bunch of rich Family members. These people control the money flow and they reward the writers, actors, and directors in ways that ensure, outside of the odd children's film or two, that what gets up on the screen remains simpatico with the System. The Family thrives in a world of violence and duality, no doubt they are familiar with the research on modelling and motor neurons, and so this is what they put up on the screens.[240]

Of course, this could change. Some members of the Family could realize the need, they could start producing scripts that model different behavior and a different reality, and they could lead a global media transformation and a global shift in consciousness. If they did, what a change that would be. In the best utopian vision, if all the production, direction, acting, and distribution talent that is currently arranged to produce socially violent shows like Survivor, the violent claptrap of superhero movies, or even Star Wars, was suddenly shifted to present images of cooperation, teamwork, and even spiritual evolution, then the brains that reflect our consciousness, and the world that we act in and create, would come to slowly reflect these

---

[239] Michael Sharp and Kiko Ellsworth, "Kinnect,"(2016).

[240] It should be noted that it is not just mainstream media that presents images of duality, conflict, and violence. Independent and smaller initiatives also represent old energy archetypes, despite their sometimes explicitly stated objectives to move beyond and offer something different.

images as well. It would take some time, and it would require other work and effort as well (like educating the population about money, changing archetypes, evolving values, and so on), but modelling cooperation, compassion, goodwill, friendly competition, and spiritual evolution in the mass media 'verse would be an important contribution to a global shift and the salvation of the world.

USE YOUR DISCERNMENT

And that's really all I have to say. I just want to end this little treatise on the economy with these final words—use your discernment! There are a lot of people offering advice, guidance, and analysis out there these days and a lot of them are pretty clueless when it comes to workable, aligned alternatives. My advice to you is, do your research, but be critical. Keep an open mind, but come to your own conclusions. Mostly important, keep in mind the basic lesson of this essay, which is that we have to understand the nature of money before we can make any valid changes. Any authentic solution to the crises at hand must include an awareness of the nature of money and the problems with accumulation. If that is missing, if people talk about God or faith or climate change or terrorist interventions or whatever their particular issue is, but they do not talk about the problems with money and accumulation, their solutions are probably unreasonable and untenable because they lack grounding in the critical financial realities of this planet. This is key. Nothing on this planet is going to get fixed until we wake up, see the problem (i.e. money, accumulation, and debt), and fix it at its root. When you boil it right down to essence, our major problem isn't technology, ignorance, hatred, zealotry, war, superstition, evolutionary selection, or anything like that. Our problem is that we have been confused about the nature of money, and passive in the face of out of control accumulation. If we are going to save the planet, that has to stop. Therefore, and at the risk of beating a dead horse, any solutions to the downward spiral must come with sophisticated understanding of money, debt, and the global problems caused by a centuries old accumulation regime that is, as is becoming increasingly obvious, destroying humanity and the planet we inhabit. Ungrounded discussions of "attraction", zeitgeist ramblings about technological salvation of this world, pretentious meetings of world representatives of the System, or presidential pats on the back about all the progress we are making, do not amount to a sniff of snot unless they are contextualized within an authentic understanding of money, accumulation, and the problems wrought on the planet by an out of control regime of accumulation. Without an awareness of this critical variable it is all just smoke and mirrors.

Keep this in mind. *We have been fooled before; we cannot afford to be fooled again.*

January 21, 2016

On reaching Jerusalem, Jesus entered the temple area and began driving out those who were buying and selling there. He overturned the tables of the money changers and the benches of those selling doves, and would not allow anyone to carry merchandise through the temple courts. And as he taught them, he said, "Is it not written: My house will be called a house of prayer for all nations? But you have made it a den of robbers." The chief priests and the teachers of the law heard this and began looking for a way to kill him, for they feared him, because the whole crowd was amazed at his teaching. **Mark 11: 15-18**.

AFTERWORD –
A RETURN TO HEGEL

> To be grateful...to Marx for his inversion of the Hegelian dialectic in the interest of an empirical understanding of human affairs does not preclude the possibility that...one might once more stand Marx on *his* head.... Put simply, this would imply that man projects ultimate meanings into reality because that reality is, indeed, ultimately meaningful. Peter Berger, 1969: 180).

This book is about money. More to the point, this book is a revelation about the nature and purpose of money. This might sound like a big deal but really it is not. As we see in the body of this work, there is nothing particularly esoteric or complicated about money. Despite the fact that economics texts usually do a horrible job of trying to define money, if they even bother at all, money is a simple thing. Money is abstracted labor pure and simple.

Being about money, this book is also, necessarily, a criticism, not of money per say, but of the general misuse and exploitation of money. Money is a potent means of economic exchange; but it is also easy to accumulate, and the easy way you can pile money in a mattress, lock it away in a vault, or represent it as a series of numbers, makes it a peculiar and pernicious ally of greed, graft, and corruption. As we see, the accumulation of money is the root of the world's evil. It is the easy way that money can be accumulated that has brought us to the brink of ecological and social disaster.

Having made this book a criticism of money is not to suggest that we need to replace money. I do not propose, as some others, that we should eliminate money, replace it with "free everything," or develop gold or resource standards of value. None of the typical solutions would work anyway because not only are they based on a profound misunderstanding of the nature of money, a misplaced sense of the root of the problems, but they are hopelessly naïve as well. On the contrary, this book is written in honour of money, and recognizes money as the motor of modern economic development, and the foundation of an advanced modern society. Unless we are content to be a world of takers, we must always exchange our labor in a fair and equitable fashion, and for that there is nothing better than money. Indeed, it is my belief that money, properly regulated, is the foundation of a future utopia. Therefore, this book argues that we should embrace money for the wonderful gift that it is, but fix the problems that money has caused.

As we see in this books, money has caused some problems. Money is powerful, but it is also dangerous. Money, or rather love of money leading to its accumulation, has been the root of centuries of suffering, violence, greed, graft, distortion, and corruption. In our day and age we are rapidly reaching an environmental and social wall. Global warming, high rates of psychological distress in the West, obscene levels of economic inequality, suffering, global violence, and a cyclic and deepening economic crisis lead me to conclude that we either change the way we do things, or we go down with the proverbial ship. And I do not think having a lot of money in the bank is going to help very much when the ship goes down. If the food supply collapses because of a toxic meltdown in the environmental balance, the world as we know it goes away and all the money in the world won't bring it back because, as you understand by the end of this book, all the money in the world is useless unless you have somebody to give it to.

Important to note, because this book is short I cannot do more than point to the problems, but I do not feel there is a need to lay out a preachy and laborious tome detailing the long list of problems we face. In this age of Internet connectivity, anybody with eyes, and a modicum of sensibility, can see the problems. The main purpose of this book is simply to link awareness of the problems with awareness of the true root of the problem, which is not human genetics, internalized pathology, essential evil, Darwinian violence, or failed evolution, but money. As we see money, money, money (or rather the love of money) is the root of all evil.

Now, I am not the first one to do something like this. Karl Marx wrote a multivolume treatise on money entitled *Das Capital*. In that book Marx pointed out the nature of money and all the distortions to which it was given. He saw the suffering and he understood the root. Marx completed a profound exposure of money. It was an exposure that must have disturbed and upset him deeply because after writing it he felt the only *solution* to the problem of money was a bloody proletarian revolution. The history of the world is the history of class exploitation, he said, and the worker must rise up and put down the ruling elites! Of course, as we know, the proletarian revolution failed. The proletarian revolution, like the French revolution, didn't solve the problem of money, it only changed the people who were accumulating it, and perpetuated the violence of elite rule over working class slaves. Instead of rich Russian monarchs oppressing peasants we had rich Russian bureaucrats oppressing workers (and now, with the transition to Capitalism, rich Russian capitalists oppressing workers). Despite calls for change, the song has remained the same.

It is not surprising to me that Marx's call for revolution failed. You can't make new friends while riding a spitting camel and *you can't teach and instruct the masses with an obtuse three-volume tome.* You also can't beget a new system with violence, because when you found a new society on violence, violent people move in and take over, and that is no good for anybody. This is the lesson of the Communist Revolution in Russia. It created a society founded on violence, rooted it in violence, and it became violent at all levels. Of course Capitalism is no better in this regard. The point here is not to point fingers, but to simply say there are no violent solutions to the problem of money, ever.

Still, consideration of solutions is necessary. By the end of this book you hopefully see the problem. When you do, questions about solutions are naturally invoked. What are we going to do about the problem, because it is a problem. If we leave it unattended we get George Orwell's surveillance and control nightmare, *1984,* in the interim, and an economic train wreck in the foreseeable future. Let the train run its course, the damage will be extensive, and the rich and poor will suffer alike. Those sitting in first class die first when the train hits the wall.

So what is the way forward? Personally I feel the solution is to be found in the breaking of barriers and the elimination of separation. We can't move forward while we are at each other's throats. We all have to realize we are all in this together and as such we have to work together to find the solution. But how is that going to happen? How do you convince the rich person to change the rules in a way that ultimately undermine their wealth, and how do you convince the working class, once they clue in to the truth, to put down their sticks and stones and let bygones be bygones.

The reality is, you can't do that within current spiritual or scientific narratives. Current spiritual and scientific narratives are hierarchical, exclusionary, elitist, and violent (I call these narratives **old energy** narratives). Current spiritual and scientific narratives are actually part of the problem, part of **the System**, that keeps the train running on the same "old energy" track. You can't refer to extant narratives them for solutions because they either encourage separation and duality, or encourage an "us versus them mentality" that does nothing but reinforce the duality and underwrite the situation. You can't go to science either. There are ideological components to science and these components, rooted as they are in the strong foundation of an empirically based biology, are difficult to shake. Science may be totally wrong about human nature[241], but science's view sticks and it will take a long time to change it. Not only that, but its view of humanity as evolving ape doesn't lend itself to hopeful utopian reverie. At the most it lends itself

---

[241] For example, biologists have long suggested that "alpha males" naturally, inevitably, and necessarily *dominate* subordinates in their species. Scientists are however beginning to recant as they themselves begin to recognize the deep ideological nature of some of their empirical stipulations. See for example Mike Sosteric, "Ding Dong the Alpha Male Is Dead," *The Socjourn* (2012).

towards subtle ideological justification of the strong dominating the weak. Like traditional spiritual narratives it supports the world we currently live in, and since the world we currently live in seems to be in increasingly dire straits, it is of no practical help at all.

So what do we do?

The long answer is that we have to develop new narratives and new ways of conceiving humanity. We need a new spirituality and a new science. Here I would turn back to Hegel for some clues to an appropriate narrative. Hegel, an absolutely brilliant German historian, and mentor of Karl Marx believed that humans were part of a bigger picture and that despite all our greed, graft, violence, and corruption we all worked on a bigger "plan." Hegel did not feel that history was a random collection of events. Hegel, not a stupid man, saw rhyme and reason in history. At the risk of invoking knee-jerk rejection here, Hegel saw God unfolding in history,[242] but not what most people might think of as God. For Hegel, God's essence was FREEDOM. The purpose of history, the purpose of humanity, was the gradual understanding of the nature and essence of this freedom, and the gradual manifestation of this freedom in the polity of the people, a manifestation that would occur as a dialectical swing of history *brought humanity towards ever more precise realizations of the underlying historical Geist.* Hegel saw human history as a gradual and inexorable movement from bondage toward freedom. He rejected the noble savage view of things (i.e.

---

[242] G.W.F. Hegel, *The Philosophy of History* (New York: Dover Publications, 2004),

http://www.marxists.org/reference/archive/hegel/works/hi/.

the view that we had a utopian past) and pointed out bondage to the environment and to subsistence as the antithesis of freedom. We are not free to do what we please while we are bound to subsistence labor twenty-four seven. At the risk of being accused of putting words into Hegel's mouth, if we want freedom we need an environment, a technological infrastructure, a polity, an economy, and an archetypal system devoted to this ideal.

For Hegel it was the realization in thought, and the manifestation in reality, of the reality of freedom, the reality of God, that was the telos of human history. According to Hegel, humans struggled to realize this lofty goal. Humans struggled not only to understand freedom, to make it a part of their thinking, but also to actuate it. This gave history a trajectory and, more importantly, an end point. At some point freedom would be actuated and history, as the working out of God's Idea, would end in full realization of the Idea in reality. It is a utopian perspective yes, but is it far more common, even in the hallowed hallways of science, than you might at first think.[243]

Of course, looking at history, and even looking at our current situation, we can see there is a problem. How do you square the rampant inequality, global crises, and

_____

[243] See for example Noble, *The Religion of Technology: The Divinity of Man and the Spirit of Invention*. Noble does a brilliant job of identifying the spiritual geist in industrial and post-industrial science. Also notable in this regard is the science fiction writing of Arthur C. Clarke, and in particular in book Childhood's End. Arthur C Clarke, *Childhood's End* (New York: Del Rey, 1987).

psychologically and emotionally oppressive strategies of today's governments (indeed of any government past or present) with a grand and glorious telos? Hegel did that in a simple and elegant way by making the content of human history, a content filled with greed, graft, corruption, inequality, self-interested passion, and instinctual gratification, **the motor that drives us forward**. According to Hegel we needed to be motivated to work. More to the point, humans (or as I would say, the *human physical unit)* didn't do anything unless it was motivated by selfish interest and passion. As he says, "We assert ... that nothing has been accomplished without an interest on the part of those who brought it about. And if 'interest' be called 'passion' – because the whole individuality is concentrating all its desires and powers, with every fibre of volition, to the neglect of all other actual or possible interests and aims, on one object – we may then affirm without qualification that nothing great in the world has been accomplished without passion."[244]

For Hegel human self-interest and passion was what drove the history of this world. Hegel would say that yes, it appears, on the surface, that we are just these violent apes, these unwashed masses, the greedy and powerful "great men" and women, but underneath it all we are really working on the same thing, the realization of Freedom. God has created conditions whereby humans are driven to

[244] Georg Wilhelm Freidrich Hegel, Reason in History, a General Introduction to the Philosophy of History, (Liberal Arts Press, 2015),
https://www.marxists.org/reference/archive/hegel/works/hi/intro duction.htm.

manifest the freedom of God. The history of the world, says Hegel, is the history of a growing global Freedom driven forward, in an admittedly counterintuitive way, by greed and selfish self-interest of a divinely driven human being.

Now Hegel had some interesting things to say about the conditions of Freedom, and I want to add some things to Hegel. Most important was that Hegel saw a strong *state* as the essential prerequisite of Freedom. People would always be engaged in self-interested behaviors thought Hegel; it was the nature of the beast. However, a strong government, i.e. a strong state, could manage and harmonize competing interests and create conditions whereby the freedom of one person did not overrule the freedom of another. The goal of Freedom, and the political precursor to advanced spirituality was, contrary to the neo-con view, a strong state. It was an essential feature. It is worth letting Hegel speak for himself here.

> From this comment on the second essential element in the historical embodiment of an aim, we infer – considering for a moment the institution of the state – that a state is then well constituted and internally vigorous when the private interest of its citizens is one with the common interest of the state, and the one finds gratification and realization in the other – a most important proposition. But in a state many institutions are necessary – inventions, appropriate arrangements, accompanied by long intellectual struggles in order to find out what is really appropriate, as well as struggles with private interests and passions, which must be harmonized in difficult and tedious discipline. When a state reaches this harmony, it has reached the period of its bloom, its excellence, its power and prosperity. But world

history does not begin with any conscious aim, as do the particular circles of men. Already the simple instinct of living together contains the conscious purpose of securing life and property; once this primal society has been established, the purpose expands. But world history begins its general aim – to realize the idea of Spirit – only in an implicit form (an sich), namely, as Nature – as an innermost, unconscious instinct. And the whole business of history, as already observed, is to bring it into consciousness.[245]

I have to agree with Hegel here that a strong state is necessary, at least in transitional stages; not the kind of state they had in Russia in its known modern history, but the kind of pluralistic and democratic state that ensures the interests of all groups are met. We need a pluralistic democracy and a participatory state. It's not something we have now. Now we have a state controlled by a single group of people (the rich and powerful). We have a situation where the power of the state is used not to further the interests of God and Freedom, but a state used in the service of private interests and accumulation. This is not necessarily a bad thing, at least according to Hegel. According to Hegel history moves like a swinging pendulum, from thesis to anti-thesis and back again, always moving forward, always leading to greater understanding, and always lifting us up to the lofty telos of Freedom. If Hegel is right, at some point we'll all wake up to the truth, realize the situation, swing left on the pendulum, and use our experiences and insight to build the state that we need, that we are driven, to build.

---

[245] Ibid.

Beyond the development of a plural and truly democratic state, I think there are other requirements of Freedom. Education is one. We need to educate each new generation to high standards of wisdom and insight. Educating the masses has always been a problem of course. On the one hand, education is arguably an arm of the social class system with the working class being trained into subservience, and higher classes being trained into rulership.[246] In this context, proper education means wresting control from the elites who control it. On the other hand, it costs money to educate and so education (at least higher education) has always been something that only people with a certain amount of money can enjoy. That's changing though. Technology has reached a point where mass education of the planet is possible. As an educator myself I can see the global potential of Moodles, Moocs, and Soocs[247] to wrest control of the education process, smash the barriers, and bring education to the masses thereby elevating the planet like never before. The potential is there. We live at the cusp of a profound revolution, but not a violent one.

Technology is another requirement of Freedom. Hegel noted that bondage to subsistence did not a freeman make, but neither did bondage to factories, or offices, or boardrooms. If humanity wants to be free to pursue its passions, the basic tasks of survival, the basic foundation of prosperity, has to be technological. Technology has to be

---

[246] Jean Anyon, "Social Class and the Hidden Curriculum of Work," *Journal of Education* 162, no. 1 (1980).

[247] For more on MOOCs, see the Wikipedia entry. https://en.wikipedia.org/wiki/Massive_open_online_course

developed to a point where the human race as a totality can be freed from the bondage of substance. That point has been reached. We live in a world where our technological prowess is enough to free the world from the bitter bondage of production. Factories and farms would still exist, but the need for long hours, sweatshop conditions, and economic bondage no longer hold. The only thing that maintains us in the vicious cycle is the continuation of regimes of accumulation. The workweek can be reduced, unnecessary activities can be dropped, and the world can be brought forward into a realm where work no longer serves the interest of accumulation, and labor is no longer alien and alienating.

State, education, and advanced productive technology—it is the development of these to the point of perfection/*alignment* that brings us to the bloom of Spirit and the end of history. The only problem is that money is easy to accumulate and this *accumulation of money,* which is also the accumulation of labor as we have seen in the main body of this essay, has led us into temptation. Not that accumulation *per se* is a bad thing. Big fat bank accounts allow capitalists to invoke massive capital projects, and these capital projects are an essential feature of a free and modern world. But accumulation is

a) out of control and
b) organized for private aggrandizement and not public benefit.

In the swing of the pendulum to the right we can see the benefits of being able to abstract, control and accumulate labor, but the arc and anti-thesis has been reached and we either swing back to the middle and end the cycle (i.e. stop swinging back and forth and step off the "checkerboard"), or we smash the train against the wall.

The question before us now is, how do we move forward from this point? I think at this point we have reached the end of history and so now the only thing for us to do is wake up, understand the Idea, actuate the full potential, and finally and forever stop the pendulum swing. And I have to say that we all have a part to play, and a decision to make. Rich or poor, black or white, male or female, we need to make a choice. We can either stay on the pendulum swing of history, moving back and forth between thesis and anti-thesis, good and evil, light and dark, struggling in that way we do to live the best life we can, or we can step of the **Wheel**[248] and actuate utopia. If we choose to stay on the Wheel, then I fear the denouement is close at hand. Remnants of humanity may continue on, but the progress we have made will be figuratively and literally submerged[249] by the ecological, emotional, and psychological disasters that loom just ahead. On the other hand, if we choose to move forward, to admit the telos and

---

[248] *The Wheel* is an old energy archetype that suggests life is a randomly spinning karmic/cosmic/evolutionary cycle of good and bad, ups and down, fortune and misfortune. For more see http://spiritwiki.lightningpath.org/The_Wheel

[249]Coastal regions are already in jeopardy, and many houses will become unliveable within a 30-year mortgage cycle! Mass exodus from flooding coastal regions will begin to occur as soon as banks stop providing mortgages to people who want to buy houses on the coast! This may occur in as little as 5 years.

See See Russ Zimmer, "Scientist: Barrier Islands Could Be Unlivable in 50 Years," *USA Today*2016.

see **"The Plan"**, then we can step off the Wheel, focus our attention on the problem (i.e. accumulation and debt) and, with a wave of the magical legislative wand, fix it and usher in utopia for all.

Ridiculous?

Balderdash?

Hopelessly naïve?

Foolishly utopian?

Certainly if one believes the propaganda, it is. If history is the random result of evolutionary chance, if we are apes emerging out of a violent and competitive past, if we are hopelessly dashing ourselves against a natural world devoid of reason and rationality, if we are ejected sinners, if we are unworthy peons of a totalitarian cosmic order, there is no hope. If this is the case, then the best we can do is hang on to dwindling hope that our "leaders" are able to mitigate the growing damage, and continue to be able to functionally support global economies despite the growing weight of debt and disaster. On the other hand, if history is more than mere random chance, if we aren't savage apes engaged in empty evolution, if we aren't mere ejected sinners, or karmic rejects, if there is something more that we are working towards, if there is (a la Hegel) an end to history, then maybe we can point to the world as it is now, where the technological and economic infrastructure of society is capable of delivering global satisfaction and utopia, and say this is that point, if we but make the right choice.

Personally, I prefer the "end of history" option. Personally, I prefer the notion of geist, though I have to say I am not a fan of the dialectic, which I think is just elite propaganda. I am going to go out on a limb here and say, we are at the end of history. What we have to do now is wake up and see the plan. We have to recognize we are all in the same boat and working towards the same goal, or we are going to sink plain and simple. Returning to the idealism of Hegel is a move in the right direction. Extending Hegel's narrative, and the narrative of others, in an inclusive, democratic, egalitarian, and free direction, and eliminating old energy ideas and archetypes that continue to support the "basis of exploitation",[250] is the work ahead.

Of course, there will be objections. When Marx stripped Hegel's dialectical process of the *geist* and made the dialectic a vacuous technical process, his criticisms were valid. For all his brilliance, Hegel was a bit short sighted in some areas. He viewed religion and the state as quintessential expressions of the Plan,[251] but conveniently ignored the fact that religion and the state can be made to function like weapons against the poor.[252] Religion is the opiate of the masses, the state is an agent of class oppression, and the history of the world is the history of class struggle. Similarly, some of his views of Spirit miss the mark, and by a long shot. Hegel was blind to the abuses of religion and power and many people are blind to the immaturity and silliness of their own spiritual faiths. But

---

[250] I speak about the "basis of exploitation" and the need to revise our ideas and archetypes in the main body of this essay.

[251] Hegel, *The Philosophy of History.*

[252] Marx, *A Contribution to the Critique of Hegel's Philosophy of Right,* "The German Ideology," in *The Marx-Engels Reader,* ed. R. Tucker(New York: Norton, 1978).

does this mean there is nothing there, or that science cannot investigate, or that the verdict is conclusively in favour of an empty physical 'verse? Not by a long shot. Spirituality, religion, philosophical thought about the essence of our reality may often miss the mark and be about everything but what they profess to be about, but there is something there worth investigating, and I'm not the first academic to say it.[253] Hegel said there was something "behind history" and it may very well be that *proper apprehension and expression, followed by cooperative manifestation and actuation* of whatever it is that is behind history, is the only way off the sinking ship.

Proper apprehension and expression of the *Geist* is way beyond the scope of this work. This work is about money and the goal of this *Rocket Scientists' Guide to Money and the Economy: Accumulation and Debt* is simply to reveal the nature of money, the root of our collective troubles, and the simple solution. And really our problem here isn't the solution, because as noted in the main text of this essay, that's easy. The problem is convincing everybody that we need to put aside our differences and work together to implement the solution and bring history to its inevitable end. And please understand, there is no violent solution here. Forcing ourselves upon people and taking things from them violently only leads to more violence, the antithesis of Freedom and happiness. Violence means another

---

[253] James, *The Varieties of Religious Experience: A Study of Human Nature*; A. H. Maslow, "Cognition of Being in the Peak Experiences," *The Journal of Genetic Psychology* 94(1959); Carlos Castaneda, *The Teachings of Don Juan: A Yaqui Way of Knowledge, 40th Anniversary Edition*(New York: Washington Square Press, 1996).

tortuous and century long swing of the pendulum, and I do not think we'll survive that swing, at least not in a way that any of us would find enjoyable. Therefore, it comes down to a question of voluntary choice. Having been presented with the issues clearly and having seen "the light", the question is, what are you going to do? Do you put this book in a corner, pretend you didn't read it, and continue on in the old ways hoping that random evolutionary advance, or divine salvation from above, is going to save this sinking ship; or do you, rich or poor, black or white, male or female, embrace the solution, embrace your power, and make the changes you need to make. There's no point in shooting the messenger! Personally I do not care what choice you make, because it is your conscious you have to deal with. I will say this: if Hegel was right, if there is an underlying movement to history, and if this movement is as powerful and inexorable as it must be to have brought us to this point, then I can say with a certain degree of confidence that resistance is probably futile. If the time has come to end history, the *Geist* will find a way and you can either swim over to the new ship and get on board with the program or, rich or poor, black or white, high or low, sink beneath the violent waves of an old energy reality that is rapidly crumbling away.

MS. October 26, 2015.

REFERENCES

"10 Simple Points to Help You Understand the Syria Conflict." *News.com.au*, 2013.

Acharya, Sourya, and Samarth Shukla. "Mirror Neurons: Enigma of the Metaphysical Modular Brain." *Journal of Natural Science, Biology, and Medicine* 3, no. 2 (Jul-Dec 2012): 118-24.

Anonymous. "Common Portrayals of Aboriginal People." Media Smarts, http://mediasmarts.ca/diversity-media/aboriginal-people/common-portrayals-aboriginal-people.

———. "Species Extinction and Human Population." http://www.whole-systems.org/extinctions.html.

Anyon, Jean. "Social Class and the Hidden Curriculum of Work." *Journal of Education* 162, no. 1 (1980).

Association, Canadian Medical. "Health Equity and the Social Determinants of Health." Canadian Medical Association, https://www.cma.ca/En/Pages/health-equity.aspx.

Badger, Emily. "People Have No Idea What Inequality Actually Looks Like." *Washington Post*, 2015.

Balzli, Beat, and Michaela Schiessl. "The Man Nobody Wanted to Hear: Global Banking Economist Warned of Coming Crisis." *Spiegel International* (July 08 2009).

Bandura, A. *Social Learning and Personality Development*. New York: Hold, Rinehart & Winston, 1963.

Bass, Kyle. "Hayman Capital Letters." Hayman Capital Management, 2012.

Beniger, James R. *The Control Revolution: Technological and Economic Origins of the Information Society*. Boston: Harvard University Press, 1989.

Berger, Peter. *The Sacred Canopy: Elements of a Sociological Theory of Religion*. New York: Anchor Books, 1969.

"Bilderberg Group." Wikipedia, https://en.wikipedia.org/wiki/Bilderberg_Group.

Blackburn, Robin. *Ideology in Social Science: Readings in Critical Theory*. Glasgow: Fontana, 1975.

Bland, Bill. "Stalin: The Myth and the Reality." Marxists Internet Archive, https://www.marxists.org/archive/bland/1999/x01/x01.htm.

Bohm, David. "Postmodern Science and a Postmodern World." In *The Reenchantment of Science*, edited by David Ray Griffin, 57-68. New York: State University of New York, 1988.

———. *Wholeness and the Implicate Order*. London: Routledge Kegan Paul, 1980.

Bourque, Linda Brookover. "Social Correlates of Transcendental Experiences." *Sociological Analysis* 30, no. 3 (Fall1969 1969): 151-63.

Bourque, Linda Brookover, and Kurt W. Back. "Language, Society and Subjective Experience." *Sociometry* 34, no. 1 (1971): 1-21.

Bowman, Gary E. "Einstein and Mysticism." *Zygon: Journal of Religion & Science* 49, no. 2 (2014): 281-307.

Braverman, Beth. "This Is a Big Problem for the Auto Industry – and It's Getting Worse " *The Fiscal Times*, January 19 2016.

Buchheit, Paul. "Infuriating Facts About Our Disappearing Middle-Class Wealth." Moyers and Company, http://billmoyers.com/2014/11/04/infuriating-facts-disappearing-middle-class-wealth/.

Buffet, Warren E. "A Minimum Tax for the Wealthy." *New York Times*, 2012.

Bühler, George. "The Laws of Manu." Sacred-Texts.com, http://www.sacred-texts.com/hin/manu.htm.

Busky, Donald F. *Democratic Socialism: A Global Survey*. Westport, CT: Praeger, 2000.

Castaneda, Carlos. *The Teachings of Don Juan: A Yaqui Way of Knowledge, 40th Anniversary Edition*. New York: Washington Square Press, 1996.

"Christopher Columbus: The Third Voyage." The Mariners' Museum, http://ageofex.marinersmuseum.org/index.php?type=explorersection&id=65.

Clarke, Arthur C. *Childhood's End*. New York: Del Rey, 1987.

Comte, Auguste. *The Catechism of Positivism; or, Summary Exposition of the Universal Religion.* London: John Chapman, 1852.

Control, Center for Disease. "Suicide among Adults Aged 35–64 Years — United States, 1999–2010." *Morbidity and Mortality Weekly Report (MMWR)* 62, no. 17 (2013): 321-25.

Cornell, Camilla. "The Real Cost of Raising Kids." *Money Sense*, June 11 2011.

Coyne, Sarah M., Simon L. Robinson, and David A. Nelson. "Does Reality Backbite? Physical, Verbal, and Relational Aggression in Reality Television Programs." *Journal of Broadcasting & Electronic Media* 54, no. 2 (2010/05/19 2010): 282-98.

Dawkins, Richard. *The God Delusion.* New York: Mariner Books, 2006.

Deangelis, Tori. "Consumerism and Its Discontents." *Monitor on Psychology* 35, no. 6 (2004): 52.

Dearing, Eric, and Beck A. Taylor. "Home Improvements: Within-Family Associations between Income and the Quality of Children's Home Environments." *Journal of Applied Developmental Psychology* 28, no. 5–6 (9// 2007): 427-44.

Decker, Ronald, Thierry Depaulis, and Michael Dummett. *A Wicked Pack of Cards: The Origins of the Occult Tarot.* New York: St Martin's Press, 1996.

Decker, Ronald, and Michael Dummett. *A History of the Occult Tarot, 1870-1970.* London: Duckworth, 2002.

Dummett, Michael. *The Game of Tarot*. London: Duckwork, 1980.

Ecklund, Elaine Howard. *What Scientists Really Think*. Oxford: Oxford University Press, 2012.

Ecklund, Elaine Howard, and Elizabeth Long. "Scientists and Spirituality." *Sociology of Religion* 72, no. 3 (2011): 253-74.

Editorial. "Notes from the Editors." *The Monthly Review* 66, no. 1 (2014).

Einstein, Albert. *Ideas and Opinions*. Broadway Books, 1995.

———. *Out of My Later Years*. Citadel Press, 2000.

———. "Religion and Science." *New York Times*, November 9 1930.

———. "Religion and Science: Irreconcilable?". *The Christian Register* (June 1948).

———. "Science and Religion." In *The Conference on Science, Philosophy and Religion In Their Relation to the Democratic Way of Life, Inc.* New York, 1941.

Ellens, J. Harold. "Introduction: The Destructive Power of Religion." In *The Destructive Power of Religion: Violence in Judaism, Christianity, and Islam*, edited by J. Harold Ellens, 1-9. Westport, CT: Praegar, 2001.

Epstein, Robert. "How Google Could Rig the 2016 Election." Politico, www.politico.com/magazine/story/2015/08/how-google-could-rig-the-2016-election-121548.

Epstein, Robert, and Ronald E. Robertson. "The Search Engine Manipulation Effect (Seme) and Its Possible Impact on the Outcomes of Elections." *Proceedings of the National Academy of Sciences* 112, no. 33 (2015): E4512-E21.

Featherstone, Richard, and Katie Sorrell. "Sociology Dismissing Religion? The Presentation of Religious Change in Introductory Sociology Textbooks." *American Sociologist* 38, no. 1 (2007): 78-98.

Feyerabend, Paul. "How to Defend Society against Science." *Radical Philosophy*, no. 11 (Summer 1975).

Forman, Robert K.S. . *Mysticism, Mind, Consciousness*. Albany: State University of New York, 1999.

Frankenberry, Nancy K. *The Faith of Scientists in Their Own Words*. New Jersey: Princeton University Press, 2008.

Freud, Sigmund. *The Future of an Illusion*. New York: Anchor Books, 1964.

Friedersdorf, Conor. "14 Specific Allegations of N.Y.P.D. Brutality During Occupy Wall Street." *The Atlantic*, 2012.

Fries, Alison B. Wismer, Toni E. Ziegler, Joseph R. Kurian, Steve Jacoris, and Seth D. Pollak. "Early Experience in Humans Is Associated with Changes in Neuropeptides Critical for Regulating Social Behavior." *Proceedings of the National Academy of Sciences of the*

United States of America 102, no. 47 (2005): 17237-40.

Gimpelson, Vladimir, and Daniel Treisman. "Misperceiving Inequality." *National Bureau of Economic Research Working Paper Series* No. 21174 (2015).

Glover, John. "Global Debt Exceeds $100 Trillion as Governments Binge, Bis Says." *Bloomberg Business* March 9 (2014).

Griffin, David Ray. "Introduction: The Reenchantment of Science." In *The Reenchantment of Science*, edited by David Ray Griffin, 1-46. New York: State University of New York, 1988.

Guendelsberger, Emily. "I Was an Undercover Uber Driver." *Philadelphia City Paper*, 2015.

Hamer, Dean H. *The God Gene: How Faith Is Hardwired into Our Genes*. New York: Anchor, 2005.

Hayes, Adam. "The Unintended Consequences of Self-Driving Cars " *Investopedia*, September 2 2015.

Hegel, G.W.F. *The Philosophy of History*. New York: Dover Publications, 2004. http://www.marxists.org/reference/archive/hegel/works/hi/.

Hegel, Georg Wilhelm Freidrich. *Reason in History, a General Introduction to the Philosophy of History*. Liberal Arts Press, 2015. https://www.marxists.org/reference/archive/hegel/works/hi/introduction.htm.

Heriot-Maitland, Charles P. "Mysticism and
        Madness: Different Aspects of the Same
        Human Experience?". *Mental Health,
        Religion & Culture* 11, no. 3 (2008): 301-25.

Hermanns, William. *Einstein and the Poet.* Boston:
        Branden Books, 1983.

Hirschler, Ben, and Noah Barkin. "A World Divided:
        Elites Descend on Swiss Alps Amid Rising
        Inequality." *Reuters News Wire*, 2016.

"How Much Does It Cost to Run for President?".
        Bangor Daily News, 2015.

"How Much Search Traffic Actually Comes from
        Googling? ." eMarketer,
        http://www.emarketer.com/Article/How-
        Much-Search-Traffic-Actually-Comes-
        Googling/1011814.

Hunsberger, Bruce, and Bob Altemeyer. *Atheists: A
        Groundbreaking Study of America's
        Nonbelievers.* New York: Prometheus
        Books, 2006.

Inman, Phillip, Graem Wearden, and Helena Smith.
        "Greece Debt Crisis: Athens Accepts Harsh
        Austerity as Bailout Deal Nears." *The
        Gaurdian* July 9 (2015).

James, William. *The Varieties of Religious
        Experience: A Study of Human Nature.*
        New York: Penguin, 1982.

Jammer, Max. *Einstein and Religion.* New Jersey:
        Princeton University Press, 1999.

Jones, Sam. "One in Every 122 People Is
        Displaced by War, Violence and

Persecution, Says Un " *The Gaurdian*, June 2015.

Jones, Tim. "The New Debt Trap: How the Response to the Last Global Financial Crisis Has Laid the Ground for the Next." Jubilee Debt Campaign, 2015.

Kain, Erik. "Could a Debt Jubilee Help Kickstart the American Economy?". *Forbes* (Oct 5 2011).

Knights, David, and Hugh Willmott. *Labour Process Theory*. London: Macmillan Press, 1990.

Krugman, Paul. "Debt Deflation in Greece." *New York Times*, July 7 2015.

LA, Pratt, Brody DJ, and Gu Q. "Antidepressant Use in Persons Aged 12 and Over: United States, 2005–2008. Nchs Data Brief, No 76.", edited by National Center for Health Statistics. Hyattsville, MD, 2011.

Lansford, J. E., K. A. Dodge, G. S. Pettit, J. E. Bates, J. Crozier, and J. Kaplow. "A 12-Year Prospective Study of the Long-Term Effects of Early Child Physical Maltreatment on Psychological, Behavioral, and Academic Problems in Adolescence." *Archives of Pediatrics & Adolescent Medicine* 156, no. 8 (2002): 824-30.

Lepp, Andrew, Jacob E. Barkley, and Aryn C. Karpinski. "The Relationship between Cell Phone Use, Academic Performance, Anxiety, and Satisfaction with Life in College Students." *Computers in Human Behavior* 31 (2// 2014): 343-50.

Levi, Ari. "Has Google Lost Control of Its Anti-Spam Algorithm." AlleyWatch, http://www.alleywatch.com/2015/09/google-lost-control-anti-spam-algorithm/.

Loewen, James W. *Lies My Teacher Told Me: Everything Your American History Textbook Got Wrong.* Touchstone, 2009.

Lomas, Robert. *The Secret Science of Masonic Initiation.* San Francisco: Weiser, 2010.

Love, Dylan. "Researchers in Kentucky Are Trying to 3d Print a Working Human Heart out of Fat Cells." *Business Insider*, 2014.

Luby, J., A. Belden, K. Botteron, and et al. "The Effects of Poverty on Childhood Brain Development: The Mediating Effect of Caregiving and Stressful Life Events." *JAMA Pediatrics* 167, no. 12 (2013): 1135-42.

Lundy, Lisa K., Amanda M. Ruth, and Travis D. Park. "Simply Irresistible: Reality Tv Consumption Patterns." *Communication Quarterly* 56, no. 2 (2008/05/09 2008): 208-25.

Marshall, Andrew Gavin. "Entering the Greatest Depression in History." *Global Research*, August 6 2009.

Martens, Willem H. J. "Antisocial and Psychopathic Personality Disorders: Causes, Course, and Remission—a Review Article." *International Journal of Offender Therapy and Comparative Criminology* 44, no. 4 (2000): 406-30.

Marx, Karl. *A Contribution to the Critique of Hegel's Philosophy of Right.* Cambridge: Cambridge University Press, 1970.

———. *Das Capital: A Critique of Political Economy.* Translated by Samuel Moore and Edward Aveling. Three vols. Vol. One, Russia: Progress Publishers, 1867.

———. "The German Ideology." In *The Marx-Engels Reader*, edited by R. Tucker. New York: Norton, 1978.

Marx, Karl, and Frederick Engels. *The Communist Manifesto.* Oxford: Oxford Paperbacks, 2008.

Maslow, A. H. "Cognition of Being in the Peak Experiences." *The Journal of Genetic Psychology* 94 (1959 Jan 01 1959): 43.

———. "The "Core-Religious" or "Transcendent" Experience." In *The Highest State of Consciousness*, edited by John White, 339-50. New York: Doubleday, 2012.

———. *Motivation and Personality (2nd Ed.).* New York: Harper & Row, 1970.

———. *Religions, Values, and Peak Experiences.* Columbus: Ohio State University Press, 1964.

———. *Towards a Psychology of Being (2nd Edition).* New York: Van Nostrand Reinhold Company, 1968.

Maslow, A.H. *The Farther Reaches of Human Nature.* New York: Viking, 1971.

―――. "A Theory of Human Motivation." *Psychological Review* 50, no. 4 (1943): 370-96.

McCracken, Harry. "Google Vs. Death." *Time*, 2013.

McNally, David. "Power, Resistance, and the Global Economic Crisis." In *Power and Resistance: Critical Thinking About Canadian Social Issues*, edited by Les Samuelson and Wayne Antony. Halifax: Fernwood Publishing, 2012.

Mech, David. "Outmoded Notion of the Alpha Wolf." Dave Mech, http://www.davemech.org/news.html.

―――. "Whatever Happened to the Term Alpha Wolf." *International Wolf*, Winter 2008.

Mech, David L. "Leadership in Wolf, *Canus Lupus,* Packs." *Canadian Field-Naturalist* 11, no. 2 (2000): 259-63.

Miller, David, and William Dinan. *A Century of Spin*. London: Pluto Press, 2008.

Morgan, Andrew. "The True Cost." 2015.

Mui, Chunka. "Will Driverless Cars Force a Choice between Lives and Jobs?" *Forbes*, December 19 2013.

Nebehay, Stephanie. "Refugee Numbers at Record Levels Globally, According to the Un." CBC, http://www.cbc.ca/news/world/un-refugee-estimates-2015-1.3371047.

Newberg, Andew, Eugene d'Aquile, and Vince Rause. *Why God Won't Go Away: Brain Science and the Biology of Belief.* edited by

New York New York: Ballantine Books, 2001.

Newberg, Andrew, and Mark Robert Waldman. *How God Changes Your Brain: Breakthrough Findings from a Leading Neuroscientist*. New York: Ballantine Books, 2009.

Newmyer, Tory. "This Is What It Costs to Run for President." *Fortune*, March 28 2015.

Nicolaus, Martin. "The Professional Organization of Sociology: A View from Below." In *Ideology in Social Science: Readings in Critical Social Theory*, edited by Robin Blackburn, 45-75. Glasgow: Fontana, 1975.

Noam, Eli M. *Media Ownership and Concentration in America*. New York: Oxford University Press, 2009.

Noble, David. *The Religion of Technology: The Divinity of Man and the Spirit of Invention*. New York: Penguin, 1999.

Ollman, Bertrell. *Alienation: Marx's Conception of Man in Capitalist Society*. Cambridge: Cambridge University Press, 1977.

Pewewardy, Cornel. "The Pocahontas Paradox: A Cautionary Tale for Educators." *Journal of Navajo Education* 14, no. 1-2 (1996): 20-25.

Posner, Gerald. *God's Bankers: A History of Money and Power at the Vatican*. New York: Simon & Schuster, 2015.

"#Prenticeblamesalbertans Goes Viral after Jim Prentice's 'Look in the Mirror' Comment." *CBC News Edmonton*, 2015.

Programme, World Food. "Frequently Asked Questions." World Food Programme, https://www.wfp.org/hunger/faqs.

Proudfoot, Wayne. *Religious Experience.* California: University of California Press, 1985.

Ramachandran, V.S. "Mirror Neurons and Imitation Learning as the Driving Force Behind "the Great Leap Forward" in Human Evolution." Edge, http://edge.org/3rd_culture/ramachandran/ramachandran_index.html.

Reason, Todd E. "Master Yoda: Freemason or Not?" Midnight Freemasons, www.midnightfreemasons.org/2012/05/master-yoda-freemason-or-not_16.html.

Research, Syrian Center for Policy. "Alienation and Violence: Impact of Syria Crisis Report 2014." United Nations, 2014.

Rizzolatti, G., L. Fogassi, and V. Gallese. "Neurophysiological Mechanisms Underlying the Understanding and Imitation of Action." [In eng]. *Nat Rev Neurosci* 2, no. 9 (Sep 2001): 661-70.

Robers, Paul Craig. "War Is Coming — Paul Craig Roberts." http://www.paulcraigroberts.org/2014/07/28/war-coming-paul-craig-roberts/.

Ronson, Jon. *The Psychopath Test: A Journey through the Madness Industry.* United Saates: Picador, 2011.

Rutter, M, and M. Rutter. *Developing Minds: Challenge and Continuity across the Life Span.* New York: Basic Books, 1993.

Ruyle, Eugene E. "Mode of Production and Mode of Exploitation: The Mechanical and the Dialectical." *Dialectical Anthropology* 1, no. 1 (1975): 7-23.

Sachs, Jeffrey D. "The Global Economy's Corporate Crime Wave." *Project Syndicate*, 2011.

Santens, Scott. "Self-Driving Trucks Are Going to Hit Us Like a Human-Driven Truck." *Medium.com*, May 14 2015.

Sharp, Michael. *The Book of Light: The Nature of God, the Structure of Consciousness, and the Universe within You.* 4 vols. Vol. one - air, St. Albert, Alberta: Lightning Path Press, 2006.

———. *The Book of the Triumph of Spirit: Healing and Activating with the Halo/Sharp System.* St. Albert: Lightning Path Press, 2013.

———. *The Book of the Triumph of Spirit: Master's Key.* St Albert, Alberta: Lightning Path Press, Unpublished.

———. *The Book of the Triumph of Spirit: Old and New Energy Archetypes.* Triumph of Spirit. St. Albert: Lightning Path Press, 2017.

———. *The Great Awakening: Concepts and Techniques for Successful Spiritual Practice.* St. Albert, Alberta, Canada: Lightning Path Press, 2007.

———. *Lightning Path Book One - Introduction to the Lightning Path*. Lightning Path Lesson Series. edited by Michael Sharp. Vol. 1, St. Albert, Alberta: Lightning Path Press, 2014.

———. *The Rocket Scientists' Guide to Authentic Spirituality*. St. Albert, Alberta: Lightning Path Press, 2010.

———. "Screwing the Population of the World: The Secret, the Law, and the Lie." *The Sociology of Religion*, 2016.

———. *The Song of Creation: The Story of Genesis*. St. Albert: Lightning Path Press, 2006.

Sharp, Michael, and Kiko Ellsworth. "Kinnect." 2016.

Sheldrake, Rupert. *Morphic Resonance: The Nature of Formative Causatoin*. Rochester, Vermont: Inner Traditions, 2009.

Sledge, Matt. "Occupy Wall Street Lawsuits Seek Justice for Arrests, Pepper Spray Two Years Later." *Huffington Post* (Sept. 18 2013).

Smialek, Jeanna. "Here's What 7 Years at Zero Rates Have Looked Like." *Bloomberg Business*, 2015.

Snyder, Michael. "16 Facts About the Tremendous Financial Devastation That We Are Seeing All over the World." *Global Research* June 29 (2015).

———. "The Bankruptcy of the Planet Accelerates – 24 Nations Are Currently Facing a Debt Crisis." *Global Research* (2015).

Sosteric, Michael. "What Is Religion?" *The Socjourn*, 2015.

Sosteric, Mike. "Ding Dong the Alpha Male Is Dead." *The Socjourn* (2012).

———. "Mystical Experience and Global Revolution." [In en]. *Athens Journal of Social Sciences* (2018).

———. "A Sociology of Tarot." *Canadian Journal of Sociology* 39, no. 3 (2014).

"Spanish Government Cracks Down on Right to Demonstrate – Security or Repression?". *Euronews*, 2015.

Spence, Peter. "The World Is Defenceless against the Next Financial Crisis, Warns Bis." *The Telegraph* (June 28 2015).

Stace, Walter Terence. *The Teachings of the Mystics*. New York: Mentor, 1960.

Stalin, J.V. "Dialectical and Historical Materialsm." Marxists Internet Archive, https://www.marxists.org/reference/archive/stalin/works/1938/09.htm.

Stark, Rodney. "On the Incompatibility of Religion and Science: A Survey of American Graduate Students." *Journal for the Scientific Study of Religion* 3, no. 1 (1963): 3-20.

———. *What Americans Really Believe*. Waco, Texas: Baylor University Press, 2008.

Stein, Ben. *In Class Warfare, Guess Which Class Is Winning*. Vol. September: New York Times, 2006.

Stewart, Emily. "How Rich Is the Catholic Church?" *The Street*, September 22 2015.

Stewart, Heather. "Beyond Greece, the World Is Filled with Debt Crises." July 11 2015.

Stringer, Lee. "We're Hiding the Homeless to Preserve the American Myth." *The Daily Beast*, 2014.

Swimme, Brian. "The Cosmic Creation Story." In *The Reenchantment of Science*, edited by David Ray Griffin, 47-56. New York: State University of New York, 1988.

Taylor, A. M. ""The Great Leveraging." in the Social Value of the Financial Sector: Too Big to Fail or Just Too Big?". *World Scientific Studies in International Economics* 29 (2014).

Taylor, Alan M. "The Great Deleveraging." In *The Social Value of the Financial Sector*, edited by Viral V. Acharya, 33-66. Hackensack, NJ: World Scientific Publishing, 2014.

Vanderklippe, Nathan. "Opposition to Thailand's Military Junta Mounts as Even Mildest Protests Shut Down." *The Globe and Mail*, 2015.

Vidal, John. "Shell Oil Paid Nigerian Military to Put Down Protests, Court Documents Show " *The Gaurdian*, October 3 2011.

Vincent, Schilling. "8 Myths and Atrocities About Christopher Columbus and Columbus Day." *Indian Country*, October 14 2013.

Vucheva , Elitsa. "European Bank Bailout Total: $4 Trillion." *Bloomberg Business*, April 10 2009.

Waite, Arthur Edward. *The Pictorial Key to the Tarot: Being Fragments of a Secret Tradition under the Veil of Divination.* London: Rider, 1911.

WashingtonsBlog. "Why We're Sliding Towards World War." Information Clearning House, http://www.informationclearinghouse.info/art icle43538.htm.

"Wealth Inequality." Inequality.org.

Weber, Max. *The Protestant Ethic and the Spirit of Capitalism.* New York: Roxbury Press, 1904 (1995).

"What Makes Us Sick." Canadian Medical Association, 2013.

Whitehead, Shannon. "5 Truths the Fast Fashion Industry Doesn't Want You to Know." *Huff Post Style*, August 19 2014.

Wicker, Bruno, Christian Keysers, Jane Plailly, Jean-Pierre Royet, Vittorio Gallese, and Giacomo Rizzolatti. "Both of Us Disgusted in My Insula." *Neuron* 40, no. 3: 655-64.

Wikipedia. "Causes of the French Revolution." https://en.wikipedia.org/wiki/Causes_of_the _French_Revolution.

———. "Divine Right of Kings." Wikipedia, https://en.wikipedia.org/wiki/Divine_right_of _kings.

———. "Foodbank." Wikipedia, https://en.wikipedia.org/wiki/Food_bank.

———. "Frederick Winslow Taylor."
https://en.wikipedia.org/wiki/Frederick_Winsl
ow_Taylor.

———. "The French Revolution."
https://en.wikipedia.org/wiki/French_Revolut
ion.

———. "Global Surveillance."
https://en.wikipedia.org/wiki/Global_surveilla
nce.

———. "Police."
https://en.wikipedia.org/wiki/Police.

Wilber, Ken. *Quantum Questions: Mystical Writings of the World's Great Physicists* New York: Shambhala, 2001.

Williams, Paul. *Operation Gladio: The Unholy Alliance between the Vatican, the Cia, and the Mafia.* New York: Prometheus Books, 2015.

Wills, John S. "Popular Culture, Curriculum, and Historical Representation: The Situation of Native Americans in American History and the Perpetuation of Stereotypes." *Journal of Narrative and Life History* 4, no. 4 (1994): 277-94.

Yamane, David, and Megan Polzer. "Ways of Seeing Ecstasy in Modern Society: Experiential-Expressive and Cultural-Linguistic Views." *Sociology of Religion* 55, no. 1 (Spring94 1994): 1-25.

Yoshikawa, H., J. L. Aber, and W. R. Beardslee. "The Effects of Poverty on the Mental, Emotional, and Behavioral Health of Children and Youth: Implications for

Prevention." [In eng]. *Am Psychol* 67, no. 4 (May-Jun 2012): 272-84.

Younglai, Rochelle. "What Are Negative Interest Rates and How Do They Work? ." *The Globe and Mail*, December 9 2015.

Zachrisson, Henrik D., and Eric Dearing. "Family Income Dynamics, Early Childhood Education and Care, and Early Child Behavior Problems in Norway." *Child Development* 86, no. 2 (2015): 425-40.

Zimmer, Russ. "Scientist: Barrier Islands Could Be Unlivable in 50 Years." *USA Today*, 2016.

INDEX

ABOUT THE AUTHOR

Mike Sosteric is a Sociologist with a specialization in psychology, religion, mysticism, social inequality, and global education. After a series of dramatic spiritual/mystical experiences caused him to question the materialist foundation of modern science, he began exploring the spiritual and mystical side of life. Recognizing early the presence of elitism and patriarchy in the world's religious and "secret" traditions, he began creating a new, open system of spiritual/human development free of the opportunistic bias in old energy systems. Joined later by his life partner, the Lightning Path™ is the culmination of their research and healing work.

ABOUT THE LIGHTNING PATH

The Lightning Path™ (or simply LP for short) is a modern system of human development that provides you with all the information you need to heal, awaken, empower/activate, and connect (a.k.a. ascend) to the powerful Consciousness that resides within you. The LP is sophisticated, powerful, logical, grounded, rational, intellectually and metaphorically rigorous, politically sophisticated, empirically verifiable, authentic, effective, and accessible to everyone regardless of race, class, or gender.

http://www.lightningpath.org